Rock
Voices

Rock Voices

The Best Lyrics of an Era

Edited with text by
MATT DAMSKER

ST. MARTIN'S PRESS New York

Copyright © 1980 by Matt Damsker
All rights reserved. For information, write:
St. Martin's Press, Inc., 175 Fifth Ave., New York, N.Y. 10010.
Manufactured in the United States of America

Library of Congress Cataloging in Publication Data
Main entry under title:

Rock Voices.

   1. Rock music—Texts. I. Damsker, Matt.
ML54.G.R6   784.5'405   80-19181
ISBN O–312–68790–7
ISBN O–312–68791–5 (pbk.)

Designed by A. Christopher Simon

This book is for my wife, Lori,
who makes everything possible; and with love to Mom and Dad . . .

Acknowledgments

To all the songwriters represented here, thank you for writing the songs; and to all the neighbors and allies who assisted my research and preparation, some grateful acknowledgment: To Bob Miller at St. Martin's, who gave me the idea and nursed it along; to Don Silver at Arista Records, who put in the good word; to Nessa Forman, Ernie Schier, B. Dale Davis, and B. A. Bergman, for encouragement and understanding; to Irv Rubin and Annette Peacock, who made things easier; to Tom DiNardo, ever helpful; to Kal Rudman, ever GO-RILLA; to Ed Sciaky, archives NON PAREIL; to Denny Horn at Peaches, gratefully undead; to Barbara Pasquarella and Marie Thruston, at the last minute; to J. Gary Brown, who knows the words; to Jeff, Ruth, Jason, Keith, David, for love; and in memory of Scott Zucker, who loves the music, and Jerry Haber, who is proud of this, I know.

Contents

Introduction

Compiling a critic's choice of great rock lyrics may be done as logically and systematically as one might catalogue pre-Columbian artifacts or digital watches. And yet rock is probably the least logical art form we have, so I've spurned the dry temptations of logic and system in favor of a more instinctive approach. The lyrics presented in this book were chosen from memory, the philosophy being that if I can't recite a poem from memory what business have I telling people it's great? While I suspect only poets will agree wholeheartedly, the fact remains that even the most open-minded critic argues best for what he likes best (to subvert a cliché: "I know a lot about art, but I *know* what I like"). These lyrics are the ones that have been rattling around in my head and informing my most allusive conversation ever since I encountered them. I present them to you, with commentary, as if to answer and exorcise some disembodied voices. . . .

DISEMBODIED VOICE ONE: Oh no, not another attempt at comparing rock lyrics to real *poetry!*

ANSWER: True, there is poetry and there is *poetry,* and most thinking people are timid about placing rock lyrics in the latter category, but they shouldn't be. Song lyrics usually don't read as well as poems written for the printed page, but whoever said poetry originated in print? In point of fact, *lyric* poetry is, by definition, rooted in the oral —no, *sung*—tradition of Homer. *Beowulf* and *Chanson de Roland* were sung long before Gutenberg got hold of them, but we tend to forget that, preferring to relegate poetic classicism to an elitist, bookbound plateau, to call it page-poetry. As David Morse points out so well in a small, inspired volume entitled *Grandfather Rock,* the marvelous thing about the rock music of the mid- and late-1960s is that it served to return poetry—in all its allusive complexity and meta-phoric rapture—to the populist realm of the sung. What makes the poetry of '60s and '70s rock so important is that the best of it stands up relatively and surprisingly well to the best of modern page-poetry.

DISEMBODIED VOICE TWO: You're telling me that rock lyrics, which you can hardly hear anyway over all that noise, are better than the lyrics to the great standards by Irving Berlin, the Gershwins, Cole Porter? C'mon!

ANSWER: Let's just say they have more to say. The fact that a generation remembers these rock lyrics so vividly and quotes them as eruditely as their elders may quote Shakespeare, proves nothing much, except that these lyrics don't merely glisten and flow with the pure inspired craftsmanship of, say, "I Get a Kick Out of You"; they also *mean*—the way Shakespeare *means* when he operates in the raging rhapsodies of Lear: "Lend me a looking glass. If that her breath will mist or stain the stone, why then she lives . . ." On one hand, The Bard was engaged by elemental human drama, but on the other, his words were the precious clues of time, place, and substance that make poetry real, and reality somehow more real. Is it possible, then, to quote others—contemporary bards like Bob Dylan, Joni Mitchell, Neil Young, Bruce Springsteen—and ascribe as much to them? More important, will it be possible in three hundred years?

Those are the questions that seek to qualify greatness, and they're unanswerable except to approach them as scientifically as possible. Does this line from Dylan—"Oh I awoke in anger/ so alone and terrified/ I put my fingers against the glass, and bowed my head and cried . . ."—does it *mean* as much, is it as *real* now, a dozen years later, as when Dylan wrote it (or at least published it) in 1968? I think so —as much as anything *means* and is *real,* as much as any lyric is *great;* and yes, it is *more* than "I Get a Kick Out of You" or "I'll Get By," or "Chattanooga Choo-Choo" though it is not necessarily better. For Dylan has inserted clues—"awoke in anger," "put my fingers against the glass"—that seem timeless as Lear's "looking glass . . . will mist or stain the stone."

These worlds-apart poetries are, I think, in league with one another. They are certainly not in the trim league of light verse—the league in which we'd have to place most pre-'60s popsong lyrics. The only problem with placing the lyrics of Dylan *et al* in the Big League of Great Lyric Poetry is inherent in the nature of the lyrics themselves. Most came from artists whose genius lay partly in their break from popsong tradition and in their being instinctive, rather than formal about building bridges to the tradition of page-poetry. Perhaps they fill the bill as great modern poets, but they don't ask to be taken that way any more than they insist on being viewed as "pop" songwriters. Woody Guthrie may have laid the groundwork for Dylan by writing and singing his salt-of-the-earth songs, songs rich in idiom and folk poetry, and yet Guthrie's ballads were not really pop, though they mattered more than any of the day's pop-songs. Like Guthrie, Dylan made no claims to high poetry. And like Guthrie, he avoided being made more than a folksinger, but his songs made the difference. Pop hits as well as poetic anthems, they spurred a major change in pop songwriting and lent themselves to criticism—from term papers to textbooks—in the *high art* way. (Indeed, more than one observor has noted, with appropriate irony, how *Rolling Stone Magazine*—the *New York Times* of rock journalism and criticism—has made a practice of reviewing rock *lyrics* more diligently than rock *music.*)

As much as anyone, Dylan is also responsible for creating a new consciousness among aspiring writers. Those who might have made equally good traditional poets or novelists were encouraged to now write hit songs—a lucrative prospect, certainly—and be serious, quite meaningful in fact, at the same time. A particularly good example is Leonard Cohen, represented in this volume by two songs, who has realized himself as a folk-rock songwriter well beyond his earlier reputation as one of Canada's most promising writers.

By now, it's apparent that if there's a bias to this book, it's toward Bob Dylan as the godfather of modern rock poetry. The only irony is that Dylan's great lyrics make for a more awkward page-poetry than most of the rock poetry he inspired. While it's a little early to assign, say, Bruce Springsteen a similarly important place in rock history, there's no denying that Springsteen's strongest lyrics flow more smoothly on the page than Dylan's. Does this observation lessen Dylan's poetic stature, or does it merely suggest that, by Springsteen's emergence in 1973 A. D. (After Dylan), rock songwriters had become a bit more conscious of rock's claim to high art status and tailored their efforts with poetic glory in mind? Perhaps. More to the point, it suggests that Dylan's unself-conscious lyric poetry created a new rock archetype: the visionary rock troubador whose words, though they meshed seamlessly with the music, were ultimately more important than the music.

These, then, are the songmakers who followed in the wake of such watershed Dylan songs as "Blowin' In the Wind," which ignited the folk music boom of the early '60s and sounded the call for a new honesty and significance in popular music. Even so, those seminal '60s folk lyrics are not so much the stuff of this book as are the more adventurous, expressionistic lyrics that blossomed when the folkie era finally yielded to the electric intensities of rock 'n' roll. And, by extension, to the whole sophisticated arsenal of modern pop music. When an L.A. rock group whimsically known as The Byrds recorded Dylan's "Mr. Tambourine Man" and scored a major pop hit, the age of "folk-rock" was upon us. But not until Dylan himself "went electric" for his fabled Newport Folk Festival appearance did the gong really sound. Rock, the mulatto offspring of white pop and black rhythm-and-blues, with its overt sexuality and brazen beat, had taken a giant step forward, away from the restraining holds and measured formulae of Tin Pan Alley, away even from the new style-shattering standard of Beatles-era rock 'n' roll, and onto a path of creative freedom and poetic expressiveness that even The Beatles were bound to follow.

This "folk-rock" fusion represented the alliance of folk music's older values—from the honesty and agony of the Delta blues to Guthrie's spirit of protest—with the supercharged, psychologically fragmented energy of a new, post-world war, post-nuclear age. If the 1950s had been a time of cultural convalescence—a time for playing with new technological toys, a nerve-cooling era of intellectual neutrality after utter global division and militant side-taking—then the 1960s were ripe not only for a newly divisive war—Vietnam—but for an artistic response to the legacy of so much change.

And so, many seemingly change-addled lyrics are here, those of the riddling, not quite cryptic, ballads that traced the hippie exodus and interior odysseys of the 1960s to the homecomings of the 1970s. Few of them are overtly about war or liberation, though war is certainly addressed and liberation implied on many levels; they are about people challenged by a new moral complexity and responding with a new song, a song that entertained without seeking to escape from the hard questions, a song with the richness and abstract wisdom of a lyric poem.

DISEMBODIED VOICE THREE: "Interior odysseys" my ass! Everybody knows that since the '60s, rock lyrics are *drug* lyrics!

ANSWER: Sure, it's popularly contended that much of the Dylanist revolution in pop songwriting was fought under the influence of drugs, mainly the marijuana and lysergic acid diethylamide that found its way so sensationally into the '60s youth culture. And it's true, as critic Richard Goldstein points out in his book *The Poetry of Rock,* that "turning on" with drugs "replaced making love as the major repository for code in rock," and that this coding made it possible to reach the hip record-buyer without being banned from the radio for Subverting the Youth of America. But there was always something weak in the logic that suggested you couldn't really understand or truly appreciate the imagery and intent of these "acid-rock" lyrics unless you were at least as stoned as their creators were assumed to have been when they wrote them. While it would be irresponsible to understate the role of psychedelic drugs in the emerging consciousness of a generation, it would be equally irresponsible to over-emphasize it. In the atmosphere of the '60s, it was easy enough to conclude that James Taylor was rhapsodizing about an LSD trip when he sang "gone to Carolina in my mind," or that John Lennon and Paul McCartney were advocating pure psychedelic escape when they wrote "I'd love to turn you on." But was it really that simple? In poetry, one can talk quite specifically about one thing and mean something else, or something more. Looking at them now, acid-rock lyrics do seem to reflect the "expanded consciousness" of '60s drug culture, but much more than that they reflect a timeless sense of spiritual longing, of the inexpressible in a new currency of common experience. The mass trend toward psychedelic drugs, as dangerous and destructive as it may have been, had the effect of turning people inward, perhaps as an escape from the social and moral complexities of the day, but also as a method of pursuing an inner complexity long ignored by pop culture with its traditional emphasis on superficial conformity. If the lyrics of the era hadn't related to this interior adventure, they would probably have meant somewhat less to their audience; as it is, they mean no less now, in their strangely wonderful imagery, than such immortal opium visions as, say, Samuel Taylor Coleridge's "Kublai Khan." Again, this connection to poetry's classical tradition seems natural.

In looking over the lyrics assembled here, it strikes me that the dominant theme of most of them—beyond drug-tripping, change, and modern complexity—is faith: faith in something bigger, the reality of faith from both secular and religious points of view. They weren't chosen with that theme in mind, but the "instinctive approach" has unavoidably led me there, perhaps because all lasting poetry seems bound up in these questions. I realize now that these lyrics have lodged in my brain, and perhaps in yours, not simply because they are "evocative," "romantic," or "haunting," but because their disembodied voices go a deceptively long way in nourishing the soul. And in subverting another cliche: " "It's only rock 'n' roll."

M. D.

Rock
Voices

Bob Dylan

MR. TAMBOURINE MAN

"Mr. Tambourine Man" invited the onslaught of '60s acid-rock. An uptempo anthem in which the singer puts his trust in the spirits of adventure, fantasy, ancient celebration ("I'm ready for to fade/ Into my own parade . . ."), it invokes the music of the age. The tambourine is the jangling rhythmic symbol for the "wild mercury sound" Bob Dylan once spoke of as his goal in music-making, and with this song he manages to prefigure that unique electric folk music he was about to unleash on his audience. No one could have guessed that the crown prince of '60s folksong—born Robert Zimmerman in Hibbing, Minnesota—would go from emulating the earthy protest style of Woody Guthrie to the souped-up modernism of rock 'n' roll, but Dylan managed to launch both forms into the new age.

From the outset, the "jingle jangle morning" of the lyric strikes one as awesome poetry, full of sound and wonder. We can't miss the feeling once Dylan clues us in. This is the mercurial word-spinning he seems to have inherited from an earlier Dylan, Welsh poet Dylan Thomas, whose own perfect ode to youth, "Fern Hill," with its jingle-jangle line about "the sky above the dingle starry," is somehow echoed by the lyricism of "Mr. Tambourine Man."

Recorded by The Byrds in 1965—their first hit, a folk-rock watershed—and in an acoustic version by Dylan on his album of the same year, *Bringing It All Back Home,* the song's symbolism of blind, numb, and finally ecstatic forgetfulness seemed an invitation to drugs, while the tambourine man of the title was held to be some sort of pusher. Given the increasingly psychedelic orientation of '60s youth culture, it's not surprising that the lyric inspired such narrow interpretation, but Dylan was too much the poet to mean so little. "What

1

the songs are necessarily about is illusions of time," he told me (*Circus Magazine,* December 19, 1978). "Those are the kind of songs I wanted to write, the ones that have the breakup of time, and where there is no time, where you're tryin' to make believe that life is one narrow line, or . . . let me put it another way: try to make the focus as strong as a magnifying glass under the sun . . ."

It's now easier to see just that in the poetry of "Mr. Tambourine Man." Like many of Dylan's best lyrics, this one is about surrender and faith in the larger forces of will and time, and in some ultimate liberation "far from the twisted reach of crazy sorrow," if it's about anything at all. And on the simplest, most literal level, it's just a song about a tambourine man who sounds good enough to follow.

MR. TAMBOURINE MAN

Hey! Mr. Tambourine Man, play a song for me,
I'm not sleepy and there is no place I'm going to.
Hey! Mr. Tambourine Man, play a song for me,
In the jingle jangle morning I'll come followin' you.

Though I know that evenin's empire has returned into sand,
Vanished from my hand, Left me blindly here to stand but still
Not sleeping.
My weariness amazes me, I'm branded on my feet,
I have no one to meet
And the ancient empty street's too dead for dreaming.

Hey! Mr. Tambourine Man, play a song for me,
I'm not sleepy and there is no place I'm going to.
Hey! Mr. Tambourine Man, play a song for me,
In the jingle jangle morning I'll come followin' you.

Take me on a trip upon your magic swirlin' ship.
My senses have been stripped, my hands can't feel to grip,
My toes too numb to step, wait only for my bootheels
To be wanderin'.
I'm ready to go anywhere, I'm ready for to fade
Into my own parade, cast your dancing spell my way,
I promise to go under it.

Hey! Mr. Tambourine Man, play a song for me,
I'm not sleepy and there is no place I'm going to.
Hey! Mr. Tambourine Man, play a song for me,
In the jingle jangle morning I'll come followin' you.

Though you might hear laughin', spinnin', swingin'
Madly across the sun,
It's not aimed at anyone, it's just escapin' on the run,
And but for the sky there are no fences facin'.
And if you hear vague traces of skippin' reels of rhyme
To your tambourine in time, it's just a ragged clown behind,
I wouldn't pay it any mind, it's just a shadow you're
Seein' that he's chasing.

Hey! Mr. Tambourine Man, play a song for me,
I'm not sleepy and there is no place I'm going to.
Hey! Mr. Tambourine Man, play a song for me,
In the jingle jangle mornin' I'll come followin' you.

Then take me disappearin' through the smoke rings of my mind,
Down the foggy ruins of time, far past the frozen leaves,
The haunted, frightened trees, out to the windy beach,
Far from the twisted reach of crazy sorrow.
Yes, to dance beneath the diamond sky with one hand waving
Free,
Silhouetted by the sea, circled by the circus sands,
With all memory and fate driven deep beneath the waves,
Let me forget about today until tomorrow.

Hey! Mr. Tambourine Man, play a song for me,
I'm not sleepy and there is no place I'm going to.
Hey! Mr. Tambourine Man, play a song for me,
In the jingle jangle morning I'll come followin' you.

LIKE A ROLLING STONE

This song, from Bob Dylan's 1966 album *Highway 61 Revisited,* became the raging anthem of '60s youth culture almost as soon as it appeared as Dylan's premier hit single and full-force espousal of rock instrumentation. Like "Mr. Tambourine Man" and his other borderline rock songs, it rings with compressed phrasing and expressionistic flair, but its message is unmistakable. It speaks to the children of the middle class, whose rejection of modern material values has led many of them to "drop out," but to what purpose? In addressing the sudden rootlessness of these young rolling stones, Dylan is reminding us how easily we may slip from one side of the social order to the other, and he's also suggesting, with fierce irony, that we haven't quite earned such downward mobility. It's as if the "mystery tramp" and "Napoleon in rags" we once threw dimes to and must now contend with as a matter of survival, are the honest *nobility* of the down-and-out, while we "used to ride on the chrome horse" with the thieving politicos who oppress us all. More than any other, this lyric buffs the very contradiction of the '60s youth movement and seems to prophesy its eventual fall-back upon the cushion of middle-class respectability.

LIKE A ROLLING STONE

Once upon a time you dressed so fine
You threw the bums a dime in your prime, didn't you?
People'd call, say, "Beware doll, you're bound to fall"
You thought they were all kiddin' you
You used to laugh about
Everybody that was hangin' out
Now you don't talk so loud
Now you don't seem so proud
About having to be scrounging for your next meal.

How does it feel
How does it feel
To be without a home
Like a complete unknown
Like a rolling stone?

You've gone to the finest school all right, Miss Lonely
But you know you only used to get juiced in it
And nobody has ever taught you how to live out on the street
And now you find out you're gonna have to get used to it
You said you'd never compromise
With the mystery tramp, but now you realize
He's not selling any alibis
As you stare into the vacuum of his eyes
And ask him do you want to make a deal?

How does it feel
How does it feel
To be on your own
With no direction home
Like a complete unknown
Like a rolling stone?

You never turned around to see the frowns on
the jugglers and the clowns
When they all came down and did tricks for you
You never understood that it ain't no good
You shouldn't let other people get your kicks for you
You used to ride on the chrome horse with your diplomat
Who carried on his shoulder a siamese cat
Ain't it hard when you discover that
He really wasn't where it's at
After he took from you everything he could steal?

How does it feel
How does it feel
To be on your own
With no direction home
Like a complete unknown
Like a rolling stone?

Princess on the steeple and all the pretty people
They're drinkin', thinkin' that they got it made
Exchanging all kinds of precious gifts and things
But you'd better lift your diamond ring,
You'd better pawn it babe
You used to be so amused
At Napoleon in rags and the language that he used
Go to him now, he calls you, you can't refuse
When you got nothing, you got nothing to lose
You're invisible now, you got no secrets to conceal.

How does it feel
How does it feel
To be on your own
With no direction home
Like a complete unknown
Like a rolling stone?

SAD-EYED LADY OF THE LOWLANDS

In his song-painting, Bob Dylan has viewed women from just about every emotional perspective, bitter to beatific, but nowhere does he sketch the mystic depth and breadth of womanhood as compellingly and reverently as in "Sad-Eyed Lady of the Lowlands." This epic ballad stands so far apart in tone from his other songs that there's a certain poetic justice in the fact that it took up the entire fourth side of his 1966 album *Blonde on Blonde.* Despite its awkward length, its succession of similes that threaten to topple the whole construction, its almost ludicrous opacity, this lyric is one of rock's most original poems, and one of Dylan's best. It conjures imagery that practically defies interpretation yet strikes miraculously at the most inexpressible core of love. The sad-eyed lady, with her "mercury mouth . . . matchbook songs . . . gypsy hymns," her "flesh like silk . . . face like glass," with "the child of the hoodlum wrapped up in your arm," is the poetic embodiment of all that is contradictory yet perfectly consistent about a beautiful young woman, her strength, weakness, innocence, and corruption.

On another level, it's possible to view this song as an extraordinary allegory of mid-'60s America. Some have even suggested that Dylan's sad-eyed lady is really the Statue of Liberty: "with the sea at your feet," "your hollow face," "sheet metal memory," "your silhouette when the sunlight dims." Again, it would be unwise to take such a narrow view of this lyric, and Dylan himself has kept quiet about it. But to the extent that the lyric's all-American heroine may stand for all America, the metaphor holds up and finds later, more clarified expression in John Prine's "The Great Compromise."

SAD-EYED LADY OF THE LOWLANDS

With your mercury mouth in the missionary times,
And your eyes like smoke and your prayers like rhymes,
And your silver cross and your voice like chimes,
Oh, who among them do they think could bury you?
With your pockets well-protected at last,
And your streetcar visions which you place on the grass,
And your flesh like silk, and your face like glass,
Who among them do they think could carry you?

Sad-eyed lady of the lowlands,
Where the sad-eyed prophet says that no man comes,
My warehouse eyes, my Arabian drums,
Should I leave them by your gate,
Or, sad-eyed lady, should I wait?

With your sheets like metal and your belt like lace,
And your deck of cards missing the jack and the ace,
And your basement clothes and your hollow face,
Who among them can think he could outguess you?
With your silhouette when the sunlight dims
Into your eyes where the moonlight swims,
And your matchbook songs and your gypsy hymns,
Who among them could try to impress you?

Sad-eyed lady of the lowlands,
Where the sad-eyed prophet says that no man comes,
My warehouse eyes, my Arabian drums,
Should I leave them by your gate,
Or, sad-eyed lady, should I wait?

The kings of Tyrus with their convict list
Are waiting in line for their geranium kiss,
And you wouldn't know it would happen like this,
But who among them really wants just to kiss you?
With your childhood flames on your midnight rug,
And your Spanish manners and your mother's drugs,
And your cowboy mouth and your curfew plugs,
Who among them do you think could resist you?

Sad-eyed lady of the lowlands,
Where the sad-eyed prophet says that no man comes,
My warehouse eyes, my Arabian drums,
Should I leave them by your gate,
Or, sad-eyed lady, should I wait?

Oh, the farmers and the businessmen, they all did decide
To show you the dead angels that they used to hide,
But why did they pick you to sympathize with their side?
How could they ever mistake you?
They wished you'd accepted the blame for the farm,
But with the sea at your feet and the phony false alarm,
And with the child of the hoodlum wrapped up in your arms,
How could they ever, ever persuade you?

Sad-eyed lady of the lowlands,
Where the sad-eyed prophet says that no man comes,
My warehouse eyes, my Arabian drums,
Should I leave them by your gate,
Or, sad-eyed lady, should I wait?

With your sheet-metal memory of Cannery Row,
And your magazine-husband who one day just had to go,
And your gentleness now, which you just can't help but show,
Who among them do you think would employ you?
Ah, you stand with your thief, you're on his parole
With your holy medallions which your fingertips fold
And your saintlike face and your ghostlike soul,
Who among them do you think could destroy you?

Sad-eyed lady of the lowlands,
Where the sad-eyed prophet says that no man comes,
My warehouse eyes, my Arabian drums,
Should I leave them by your gate,
Or, sad-eyed lady, should I wait?

I DREAMED I SAW ST. AUGUSTINE

As the first album recorded by Bob Dylan after his near-fatal motorcycle accident in 1966 and subsequent retreat to the rural privacy of Woodstock, New York, *John Wesley Harding* marked a turning point not only for its composer but for the music of the era as well. Released in 1968, at the height of acid-rock's psychedelic sound-swirl, it prefigured a new breed of softer, down-to-earth, country-flavored rock that seemed almost a throwback to the folkie sound of the early '60s. "The Beatles had just released *Sgt. Pepper*, which I didn't like at all," recalled Dylan in 1978 (*Circus Magazine*, December 19, 1978). "Talk about indulgence; I thought that was a very indulgent album, although the songs were real good. I just thought that all that production wasn't necessary . . . didn't figure that had anything to do with anything—the psychedelic music scene, I mean."

For Dylan, *John Wesley Harding* represented a move away from the dense lyricism and feverish imagery of his previous folk-rock in favor of a more economical, spiritually calmed style that would continue through much of his later work. "I went back and just wrote real simple songs," said Dylan, in explaining the change. "There's only two songs on the album that came the same time as the music. The rest of the songs were written out on paper, and I found the tunes for 'em later. I hadn't done that before and I haven't done that since. That might account for the specialness of that album."

From the crooning neo-country sound of his next album, *Nashville Skyline*, to the bucolic family-man stance and layered pop feel of *New Morning*, a mellowed Dylan seemed to have found peace. Not until the mid-'70s, when he began touring anew with his Woodstock music mates, The Band, would Dylan re-ignite his fire-and-brimstone side. By 1979 he would return, "born again," with God-fearing songs that owed less to the Judeo-Christian symbology he used to scattershoot through his music than to the fundamentalist spirit embodied by these lyrics. "*John Wesley Harding* was a fearful album—just dealing with fear, but dealing with the devil in a fearful way, almost," Dylan observed to Jonathan Cott, also in 1978 (*Rolling Stone Magazine*, November 16, 1978). "Everybody agrees that that was pretty different, and what's different about it is that there's a code in the lyrics and also there's no sense of time. There's no respect for it: you've got yesterday, today and tomorrow all in the same room, and there's very little that you can't imagine not happening."

Without a doubt, these songs said a lot with a little, and while the portentous rocking of "All Along the Watchtower" made it the album's best-known and most-performed song, "I Dreamed I Saw St. Augustine" struck many as its most moving lyric. A vision of faith and righteousness, fear and betrayal, it finds Dylan at the most disciplined peak of his expressiveness.

I DREAMED I SAW ST. AUGUSTINE

I dreamed I saw St. Augustine,
Alive as you or me,
Tearing through these quarters
In the utmost misery,
With a blanket underneath his arm
And a coat of solid gold,
Searching for the very souls
Who already have been sold.

"Arise, arise," he cried so loud,
In a voice without restraint,
"Come out, ye gifted kings and queens
And hear my sad complaint.
No martyr is among ye now
Who you can call your own,
So go on your way accordingly
But know you're not alone."

I dreamed I saw St. Augustine,
Alive with fiery breath,
And I dreamed I was amongst the ones
That put him out to death.
Oh, I awoke in anger,
So alone and terrified,
I put my fingers against the glass
And bowed my head and cried.

Paul Simon

THE SOUND OF SILENCE

More than any other songwriter to emerge in the '60s, Paul Simon managed to refine the rough-hewn rock-baroque energy of Bob Dylan's electrified folk style into something that reflected the engineered economy and control of more traditional pop music. For unlike most rock poets, Simon had served a crucial apprenticeship as a singer, songwriter, and song-plugger on New York's Tin Pan Alley in the '50s and early '60s, when pop-rock music was still being produced on demand as if from some vast urban song factory. When Simon and his boyhood friend, Art Garfunkel, began their legendary partnership, Simon had already gained experience in the craft and business of pop. And for this reason, the music of Simon and Garfunkel amounted to a breakthrough: sophisticated and sweetly harmonic in a pop way, it was nonetheless based in the serious folkie spirit of the early '60s. Simon's lyrics reflected a society caught in the whirl of change and moral complexity, alienated by the turbulence of events, and cut off from the symbols and self-assurance that had seemed so comforting only a few years earlier.

"Actually, Dylan was writing protest, and whatever it was, everybody had a tag," Simon told Jon Landau in a 1972 *Rolling Stone* interview. "They put a tag on the alienation. And it was a self-fulfilling prophecy, so I wrote alienation songs." The "alienation song" that heralded Simon and Garfunkel's arrival on the pop scene was, of course, "The Sound of Silence," first recorded as an acoustic ballad for their 1965 debut album, *Wednesday Morning, 3 A.M.* By the time the song hit the Top 40 as a single, however, it had been doctored with some rocking electric instrumentation for the sake of cashing in on the folk-rock sound then sweeping the charts. This turned out to be one of those rare marketing ploys that work artistically as well. For the dark electro-distortion of the rock track actually enhanced the sense of the lyrics, with their poetic suggestions of emptiness amidst clamor ("People talking without speaking") and of some mass abandonment to a dangerous technological will ("And the people bowed and prayed /To the neon god they made").

THE SOUND OF SILENCE

Hello darkness, my old friend,
I've come to talk with you again,
Because a vision softly creeping,
Left its seeds while I was sleeping,
And the vision that was planted in my brain
Still remains
Within The Sound of Silence

In restless dreams I walked alone
Narrow streets of cobblestone,
'Neath the halo of a street lamp,
I turned my collar to the cold and damp
When my eyes were stabbed by the flash of
A neon light
That split the night
And touched The Sound of Silence

And in the naked light I saw
Ten thousand people, maybe more,
People talking without speaking,
People hearing without listening,
People writing songs that voices never share
And no one dare
Disturb The Sound of Silence

"Fools" said I, "You do not know
Silence like a cancer grows.
Hear my words that I might teach you,
Take my arms that I might reach you."
But my words like silent raindrops fell,
And echoed
In the wells of silence

And the people bowed and prayed
To the neon god they made.
And the sign flashed out its warning,
In the words that it was forming.
And the sign said, "The words of the prophets
Are written on the subway walls
And tenement halls."
And whisper'd in The Sounds of Silence.

AMERICA

By the late 1960s, Paul Simon's lyric style had matured enough to shed its skin of Dylanist image-mongering and "quality literature" associations. It got down to business with more naturalistic depictions of an American spirit alienated from an indifferent and often sinister mass society. "America," from Simon and Garfunkel's 1968 album *Bookends*, conversationally conveys a feeling of distant connection to some lost national truth, and of not knowing where to find it. Is it in the "real estate here in my bag"? Or in the "pack of cigarettes/ And Mrs. Wagner's Pies," in the "Greyhound in Pittsburgh," or in the four-day "hitchhike from Saginaw"? Is it in the "spy" in his gabardine suit, the magazine, the moon rising "over an open field," the cars on the turnpike? Obviously, it's in all these things, and what the singer—"empty and aching and/ I don't know why"—is really looking for is himself somewhere inside them.

AMERICA

"Let us be lovers,
We'll marry our fortunes together.
I've got some real estate here in my bag."
So we bought a pack of cigarettes,
And Mrs. Wagner's Pies,
And walked off
To look for America.
"Kathy," I said
As we boarded a Greyhound in Pittsburgh,
"Michigan seems like a dream to me now.
It took me four days
To hitchhike from Saginaw.
I've come to look for America."

Laughing on the bus,
Playing games with the faces,
She said the man in the gabardine suit
Was a spy.
I said, "Be careful,
His bow tie is really a camera."
"Toss me a cigarette,
I think there's one in my raincoat."
"We smoked the last one
An hour ago."

So I looked at the scenery,
She read her magazine;
And the moon rose over an open field.
"Kathy, I'm lost," I said,
Though I knew she was sleeping.
"I'm empty and aching and
I don't know why."
Counting the cars
On the New Jersey Turnpike.
They've all come
To look for America,
All come to look for America.
All come to look for America.

The Beatles

ELEANOR RIGBY

It's no overstatement to say that The Beatles—John Lennon, Paul McCartney, George Harrison, and Ringo Starr, the four most famous players ever to surface on the British scene—changed the face of pop-rock with their self-created, self-performed music. They brought a new kind of Anglophile wit, harmony, and electricity to the blues-based rock which had been previously defined and dominated by American performers. Moreover, The Beatles's liberated, style-shattering image seemed to fill a leadership void for the youth who'd already seen the decade's original symbol of vitality and a "New Frontier"—President John F. Kennedy—felled by an assassin's bullets. And so it wasn't long after their pop emergence in 1964 that The Beatles felt the pressure to say much more than "yeah yeah yeah" with their impressively evolving sound. Thanks to Dylan *et al,* the poetry of folk-rock was already in full swing on the hit parade.

At one point, goes the story, John Lennon, the "smart" Beatle whose impish word play had already resulted in two published volumes, *In His Own Write* and *A Spaniard in the Works,* met Bob Dylan in New York. Soon, The Beatles's songwriting began to rise to the challenge of the folk-rock revolution. The collaborative lyrics of Lennon and McCartney, as well as the less prolific output of George Harrison, grew more personal, more suggestive, deep enough to justify the increasingly eclectic arrangements and experimentation of the music itself.

"We were held back in our development by having to go onstage all the time and do it, with the same old guitars, drums and bass. We just had to stick to the basic instruments," observed Harrison to The Beatles's official biographer, Hunter Davies. "Now that we only play in studios, and not anywhere else, we haven't got a clue about what we're going to do. If Paul has written a song, he comes into the studio with it in his head. It's very hard for him to give it to us and for us to get it."

Obviously, these insular Beatles of the late '60s were blossoming as artists. And of all the "new" Beatle songs that flourished in this period, "Eleanor Rigby," with its baroque string accompaniment and sad dignity, features the most compelling lyric. Rock critic Richard Goldstein has cited its "expression of agony through triviality" as the song's key relation to the burgeoning poetry of '60s rock, but beyond that its images imply layers of observation worthy of William Butler Yeats's stark pronouncements. Through Eleanor Rigby, who "picks up the rice/ In the church where her wedding/ Has been," or Father MacKenzie, "Darning his socks in the night/ When there's nobody there," we can sense a great deal about the consequence of the past, the imperative of the present, the limitations of the future.

ELEANOR RIGBY

Ah, look at all the lonely people.

Eleanor Rigby, picks up the rice
In the church where her wedding
Has been,
Lives in a dream,
Waits at the window,
Wearing a face that she keeps
In a jar by the door,
Who is it for?

All the lonely people,
Where do they all come from?
All the lonely people,
Where do they all belong?

Father MacKenzie, writing the words
Of a sermon that no one will hear,
No one comes near,
Look at him working,
Darning his socks in the night
When there's nobody there,
What does he care?

All the lonely people,
Where do they all come from?
All the lonely people,
Where do they all belong?

Ah, look at all the lonely people
Ah, look at all the lonely people

Eleanor Rigby died in the church
And was buried along with her name,
Nobody came.
Father MacKenzie, wiping the dirt
From his hands as he walks from the grave,
No one was saved.

All the lonely people,
Where do they all come from?
All the lonely people,
Where do they all belong?

A DAY IN THE LIFE

Released in 1967, The Beatles's album *Sgt. Pepper's Lonely Hearts Club Band* pushed rock to the peak of psychedelic trippery. The album's kaleidoscopic blend of elaborate, eccentric packaging, seemingly drug-inspired songs, and sound effects left the impressionable rock fan in a daze. With its pseudo-symphonic statements of theme, its freewheeling development and recapitulations, it set a new standard for rock albums as cohesive, conceptual works of art. But The Beatles were also signalling, almost as a contradiction, coming fragmentations: their own, for one, and that of "good ol' rock 'n' roll," which they had united in a common movement, into the arty schools of style and concept which would emerge in the '70s, after The Beatles had split up.

With *Sgt. Pepper,* '60s rock culture seemed to be entering its decadent stage, and the song that said it all—"A Day in the Life"—was tacked onto the album as an afterthought, after all the psychedelic dazzle had run its course. Indeed, this "immortal rock-poem," as critic Richard Goldstein described it, evoked images of urban despair worthy of T. S. Eliot and was a kind of album in itself, divided into three main parts (like Neil Young's similar triptych, "Broken Arrow") and punctuated by the immense, crescendoing, abruptly terminated sections of orchestral dissonance that followed the lines "I'd love to turn you on." Were they imitating the obvious connotation of those words (i.e., to take drugs) or, possibly, suggesting the enormous hopelessness of "turning on" (i.e., raising up, making good) the weight of modern life?

The lyrics were, of course, the real clues ("I was writing the song with the *Daily Mail* propped up in front of me on the piano," revealed John Lennon to Hunter Davies): they suggested that our lives had indeed been reduced to mechanics ("Woke up, fell out of bed/ Dragged a comb across my head"), that our survival had something to do with the death of our emotions, with a Dylanish acceptance of chaos, emptiness, and overkill ("I read the news today oh boy . . ./ Now they know how many holes it takes/ To fill the Albert Hall"). This lyric rings out as The Beatles's best, and the one we may still read into most deeply.

A DAY IN THE LIFE

I read the news today oh boy
About a lucky man who made the grade
And though the news was rather sad
Well I just had to laugh
I saw the photograph.
He blew his mind out in a car
He didn't notice that the lights
Had changed.
A crowd of people stood and stared
They'd seen his face before
Nobody was really sure
If he was from the House of Lords.
I saw a film today oh boy
The English Army had just won the war
A crowd of people turned away
But I just had to look
Having read the book.
I'd love to turn you on.

Woke up, fell out of bed
Dragged a comb across my head
Found my way downstairs and drank a cup
And looking up I noticed I was late.
Found my coat and grabbed my hat
Made the bus in seconds flat
Found my way upstairs and had a smoke
Somebody spoke and I went into a dream.

I read the news today oh boy
Four thousand holes in Blackburn,
Lancashire
And though the holes were rather small
They had to count them all
Now they know how many holes it takes
To fill the Albert Hall.
I'd love to turn you on.

Leonard Cohen

SUZANNE

The mystic rapture of Leonard Cohen's "Suzanne" had become something of a legend on the folk-rock scene well before Cohen recorded it on his 1968 debut album, *Songs Of . . . .* With its strangely idealized heroine whose strangeness forms the basis of her attraction, Cohen's lyric seems to capture the '60s spirit of occult romanticism as no other, and for that reason it became one of the most performed songs of its day. Now, out of its original context, the lyric stands as a timeless evocation of love, faith, and rebirth amidst confusion and decay. Cohen's metaphoric scheme haunts us with images of "tea and oranges," "garbage and the flowers," "heroes in the seaweed," of Jesus "broken/ Long before the sky would open," while Suzanne herself represents the day's "half-crazy," convention-flouting flower child in her "rags and feathers." Through her, Cohen imagines a generation of young dreamers sifting the rivers of waste and old values in search of something fresh to believe in.

SUZANNE

Suzanne takes you down to her place near the river
You can hear the boats go by
You can spend the night beside her
And you know that she's half crazy
But that's why you want to be there
And she feeds you tea and oranges
That come all the way from China
And just when you mean to tell her
That you have no love to give her
Then she gets you on her wavelength
And she lets the river answer
That you've always been her lover
And you want to travel with her
And you want to travel blind
And you know that she will trust you
For you've touched her perfect body with your mind.

And Jesus was a sailor
When he walked upon the water
And he spent a long time watching
From his lonely wooden tower
And when he knew for certain
Only drowning men could see him
He said "All men will be sailors then
Until the sea shall free them"
But he himself was broken
Long before the sky would open
Forsaken, almost human
He sank beneath your wisdom like a stone
And you want to travel with him
And you want to travel blind
And you think maybe you'll trust him
For he's touched your perfect body with his mind.

Now Suzanne takes your hand
And she leads you to the river
She is wearing rags and feathers
From Salvation Army counters
And the sun pours down like honey
On our lady of the harbor
And she shows you where to look
Among the garbage and the flowers

There are heroes in the seaweed
There are children in the morning
They are leaning out for love
And they will lean that way forever
While Suzanne holds the mirror
And you want to travel with her
And you want to travel blind
And you know that you can trust her
For she's touched your perfect body with her mind.

THE STRANGER SONG

If "Suzanne" represented Leonard Cohen's sense of romantic optimism, then "The Stranger Song," also from his 1968 debut album, represents the sense of erotic pessimism and estrangement that dominates his work. Few other song poets have been as consistent in exploring themes of personal obsession and the failures of intimacy. "I can't get beyond that," offered Cohen recently (CBS Records biography, 1979). "I don't have the confidence or the nerve or the insight to write about the vast movements of mankind, if there are such things. I don't even know. I never got out of my personal life. I apologize, but I never did . . ."

This stark lyric requires no apology from its author as it settles into a series of insistent refrains to make an important, if depressing, point: There's a distance between people—their souls, their desires —that not even the most intimate forms of acceptance can bridge. Billy Joel makes much the same observation, with considerably more wit and flair in "The Stranger," and yet Cohen's lyric seems more painfully, poignantly at the heart of the matter.

THE STRANGER SONG

It's true that all the men you knew were dealers
Who said they were through with dealing
Every time you gave them shelter
I know that kind of man
It's hard to hold the hand of anyone
Who is reaching for the sky just to surrender.

And then sweeping up the jokers that he left behind
You find he did not leave you very much
Not even laughter
Like any dealer he was watching for the card
That is so high and wild
He'll never need to deal another
He was just some Joseph looking for a manger
He was just some Joseph looking for a manger.

And then leaning on your window sill
He'll say one day you caused his will
To weaken with your love and warmth and shelter
And then taking from his wallet
An old schedule of trains, he'll say
I told you when I came I was a stranger
I told you when I came I was a stranger.

But now another stranger seems
To want you to ignore his dreams
As though they were the burden of some other
Oh you've seen that man before
His golden arm dispatching cards
But now it's rusted from the elbow to the finger
And he wants to trade the game he plays for shelter
Yes he wants to trade the game he plays for shelter.

You hate to watch another tired man
Lay down his hand
Like he was giving up the holy game of poker
And while he talks his dream to sleep
You notice there's a highway
That is curling up like smoke above his shoulder
It's curling just like smoke above his shoulder.

You tell him to come in sit down
But something makes you turn around
The door is open, you can't close your shelter

You try the handle of the road
It opens, do not be afraid
It's you my love, you who are the stranger
It is you my love, you who are the stranger.

Well, I've been waiting, I was sure
We'd meet between the trains we're waiting for
I think it's time to board another
Please understand, I never had a secret chart
To get me to the heart of this
Or any other matter
Well, he talks like this
You don't know what he's after
When he speaks like this
You don't know what he's after.

Let's meet tomorrow if you choose
Upon the shore, beneath the bridge
That they are building on some endless river
Then he leaves the platform
For the sleeping car that's warm
You realize, he's only advertising one more shelter
And it comes to you, he never was a stranger
And you say ok the bridge or someplace later.

And then sweeping up the jokers
That he left behind
You find he did not leave you very much
Not even laughter
Like any dealer he was watching for the card
That is so high and wild he'll never need
To deal another
He was just some Joseph looking for a manger
He was just some Joseph looking for a manger.

And leaning on your window sill
He'll say one day you caused his will
To weaken with your love and warmth and shelter
And then taking from his wallet
An old schedule of trains
He'll say, I told you when I came I was a stranger
I told you when I came I was a stranger.

John Phillips
and The Mamas
and the Papas

CALIFORNIA DREAMIN'

Given their terminally unwashed and mismatched image, The Mamas and the Papas seemed at best a long shot for pop stardom. On the "Mama" side, obese Cass Elliot and emaciated Michelle Phillips looked like some jokey before-and-after display, while "Papas" John Phillips and Denny Doherty were about equally scruffy, scrawny, and homely looking. And yet this unbarbershopped quartet, this rhapsody in blue denim, tent dresses, and clumpy boots, had a vocal chemistry to rival the soaring folkie sound popularized by Peter, Paul and Mary, and to unite it with the emerging rock culture.

In 1966, the motley fashion and ethereal folk-rock style of The Mamas and the Papas—which had been forged mainly by songwriter John Phillips during his days on the New York scene—reflected the "beat" romanticism of what was being redefined for the '60s as the "hippie" lifestyle. Phillips's lyrics articulated a new sense of nomadic escape—from urban blight, or from the pains of too-transitory love—and the lyric that said it all in '66 was his "California Dreamin'." Here, the vision of California as some sort of promised land is offset by the pervasive realities of life and survival in the cold, dirty cities of the East, and by a troubled sense of romantic attachment ("If I didn't tell her/ I could leave today"). The lyric hinges on an observation of stoic faith and self-denial ("You know the preacher lights the coals/ He knows I'm gonna stay") that takes the measure of the dreamer against the dream.

CALIFORNIA DREAMIN'

All the leaves are brown
And the sky is gray
I've been for a walk, on a winter's day
I'd be safe and warm, if I was in L. A.
California dreamin', on such a winter's day.

Stopped into a church
I passed along the way
Well, I get down on my knees and pretend
To pray
You know the preacher lights the coals
He knows I'm gonna stay
California dreamin', on such a winter's day.

All the leaves are brown
And the sky is gray
I've been for a walk, on a winter's day
If I didn't tell her
I could leave today
California dreamin', on such a winter's day.

Neil Young

BROKEN ARROW

Neil Young's "Broken Arrow" has been called a "mini-opera," but its three-part (three-act?) form might be better viewed as a symbol of fragmentation—the fragmentation of '60s perceptions and, more specifically, of the great but chronically unstable rock group from which the song sprang. Formed in Los Angeles during the folk-rock boom of the mid-'60s, Buffalo Springfield brought together an extremely versatile crew of young talents, but the band's polarizing visionaries were Neil Young, a brooding singer-songwriter out of Winnipeg, Ontario, and Stephen Stills, a journeyman rocker rooted mainly in the American South. Despite the youthful intensity of Young and Stills, it seems that the band's sudden success, not its legendary ego wars, is what ultimately capsized the Springfield. But in its brief time together, it did produce three exceptional albums that married crystalline strains of acoustic-folk music to a progressive sense of rock drama.

Young and Stills would later find fame, of course, as soloists and as half of Crosby, Stills, Nash and Young, a quartet whose popularity in the '70s made them the closest thing to an American version of The Beatles. But the mystique of Buffalo Springfield continues to overshadow most of the later efforts of its players. Only Young would go on to produce music of consistently classic depth, and yet none of it would prove more evocative than his best contributions to the Springfield repertoire.

For sheer poetry, "Broken Arrow," from the 1967 album *Buffalo Springfield Again*, the band's second, is Young's early masterpiece. Its haunted imagery flows from the unrealities of rock stardom ("They stood at the stage door/ And begged for a scream") to the moral conflict of youthful rebellion and escape into drugs ("His mother had told him/ A trip was a fall") and, finally, to a vision of some dark "wedding parade" that seems but a thinly veiled reference to the funeral of John Kennedy ("The black-covered caissons/ Her horses had drawn/ Protected her king/ From the sunrays of dawn"). Bridging the three verses is a chorus that portrays a defeated, crowded-out American Indian as a symbol of all that is cruel and contradictory about the hallowed American Dream. The tortuous grace of this phrase—"Could you tell that the empty-quivered/ Brown-skinned Indian on the banks/ That were crowded and narrow/ Held a broken arrow? "—is a uniquely hypnotic high point in rock poetry.

BROKEN ARROW

The lights turned on and
The curtain fell down,
And when it was over
It felt like a dream.
They stood at the stage door
And begged for a scream,
The agents had paid for
The black limousine
That waited outside in the rain.

Did you see them?
Did you see them?
Did you see them in the river?
They were there to wave to you.
Could you tell that the empty-quivered
Brown-skinned Indian on the banks
That were crowded and narrow
Held a broken arrow?

Eighteen years of American dreams,
He saw that his brother
Had sworn on the wall.
He hung up his eyelids and ran
Down the hall.
His mother had told him
A trip was a fall,
And don't mention babies at all.

Did you see him?
Did you see him?
Did you see him in the river?
He was there to wave to you.
Could you tell that the empty-quivered
Brown-skinned Indian on the banks
That were crowded and narrow
Held a broken arrow?

The streets were lined
For the wedding parade,
The queen wore the white gloves,
The county of song,
The black-covered caissons

Her horses had drawn
Protected her king
From the sunrays of dawn.
They married for peace
And were gone.

Did you see them?
Did you see them?
Did you see them in the river?
They were there to wave to you.
Could you tell that the empty-quivered
Brown-skinned Indian on the banks
That were crowded and narrow
Held a broken arrow?

POCAHONTAS

Neil Young produced a variety of striking music throughout the 1960s, from the violent, ragged mountain-rock of early and later solo albums with Crazy Horse to his more commercially tailored mid-period work on *After the Gold Rush, Harvest,* and with Crosby, Stills and Nash. But unlike virtually every other major rock figure to emerge in the '60s, Young was quick to steer off the path of pop sweetening, embellishment, and eclectic progressivism that he'd ventured onto with Buffalo Springfield and which was to continue well into the '70s. Young obviously sensed that "folk" and "rock" are differentiated only, and merely, by electricity or the lack of it. Pop, in the modern sense, is not itself music but the engineering of musical styles into a marketed mainstream. One could argue that Young has remained the only true folk-rocker of his day, avoiding the very real adulterations of pop without losing his vast popularity. Young forces his audience to see things his way; he won't aim at the ever-moving targets of the audience itself. "I'm lucky," he told Cameron Crowe in 1979 (*Rolling Stone Magazine,* February 8, 1979). "Somehow, by doing what I wanted to do, I manage to give people what they don't want to hear and they *still* come back. I haven't been able to figure that out yet."

Significantly, it is one of Young's most recent and most successful albums, 1979's *Rust Never Sleeps,* that most powerfully asserts his devotion to the purity of folk-rock. One side is all acoustic—new folk songs—while the other is pure hard-rock. As folk music, it's timeless; as rock, it challenges the vision and vitality of the "new wave" bands whose creative return to the roots of rock seems to be charting the course of the 1980s. Young, on the other hand, is a paragon of folk-rock continuity, fully in touch with past, present, and future. The lyric "Pocahontas," from *Rust Never Sleeps,* is a brilliant example of this. Its reference to the plight and symbolism of the American Indian completes a thematic line begun years before with "Broken Arrow," while its sensual, topical poetry seems to clarify, finally, the timeless connections of flesh and spirit at the heart of Young's work.

POCAHONTAS

Aurora borealis
The icy sky at night
Paddles cut the water
In a long and hurried flight
From the white man to the fields of green
And the homeland we've never seen

They killed us in our tepee
And they cut our women down
They might have left some babies
Cryin' on the ground
But the firesticks and the wagons come
And the night falls on the settin' sun

They massacred the buffalo
Kitty corner from the bank
The taxis run across my feet
And my eyes have turned to blanks
In my little box at the top of the stairs
With my Indian rug and a pipe to share

I wish I was a trapper
I would give a thousand pelts
To sleep with Pocahontas
And find out how she felt
In the mornin' on the fields of green
In the homeland we've never seen

And maybe Marlon Brando
Will be there by the fire
We'll sit and talk of Hollywood
And the good things there for hire
And the Astrodome and the first tepee
Marlon Brando, Pocahontas and me
Marlon Brando, Pocahontas and me
Pocahontas

Stephen Stills

FOR WHAT IT'S WORTH

While Neil Young may have shouldered the mantle of poet more lastingly, his stormy partner Stephen Stills has made equally important contributions to the poetry of folk-rock. As anthems go, Stills's (and the Springfield's) greatest hit must be viewed both as a strong modern poem and a key statement of the '60s—'66, to be exact. Objectively titled "For What It's Worth," and written in response to youth riots on L.A.'s Sunset Strip, this subtly eruptive song of protest, power, and paranoia asked its audience to peer through the surface of events rather than ride them. In hesitating to take sides, the lyric sounds an early note of constructivism for the rebellious youth movements of the era.

FOR WHAT IT'S WORTH

There's something happenin' here,
What it is ain't exactly clear.
There's a man with a gun over there,
Tellin' me I got to beware.

I think it's time we stop, children,
What's that sound?
Everybody look, what's goin' down.

There's battle lines bein' drawn,
Nobody's right if everybody's wrong.
Young people speakin' their minds,
Gettin' so much resistance from behind.

It's time we stop,
Children, what's that sound?
Everybody look, what's goin' down.

What a field day for the heat,
A thousand people in the street,
Singin' songs, and they're carryin' signs,
Mostly say, "Hooray for our side."

It's time we stop, hey!
What's that sound?
Everybody look, what's goin' down.

Paranoia strikes deep,
Into your life it will creep.
Starts when you're always afraid,
Step out of line, the man come and
Take you away.

We better stop, now,
What's that sound?
Everybody look, what's goin' . . .
We better stop, hey!
What's that sound?
Everybody look, what's goin' down . . .

FOUR AND TWENTY

Stephen Stills's post-Springfield alliance with David Crosby, Graham Nash, and occasionally, Neil Young, prompted some of his best and most ambitious folk-rock, and one of the most compelling of Stills's lyrics came in a brief, almost throwaway acoustic ballad from CSNY's 1970 album *Deja Vu*. "Four and Twenty" is a stark lament that, according to David Morse in his 1972 volume, *Grandfather Rock*, echoes the emptiness and lurking despair of Baudelaire's poem, "The Abyss." In describing the material poverty of his father's life and the spiritual poverty of his own, Stills neatly implies the universal inheritance of a common emptiness (as Bruce Springsteen will imply later in "Adam Raised a Cain"). He also offers clues of time and place that make it all so real and unreal—for example, "I embrace the many-colored beast." Is this just another reference to some color-mad psychedelic drug trip, or is it closer to Baudelaire's "trace the dark with nightmare, multiform, unending . . ."?

FOUR AND TWENTY

Four and twenty years ago a-comin to this life
The son of a woman and a man who lived in strife
He was tired of being poor
And he wasn't into sellin' door to door
And he worked like the devil to be more.

A different kind of poverty now upsets my soul
Night after sleepless night I walk the floor and I
Want to know
Why am I so alone?
Where is my woman
Can I bring her home?
Have I driven her away?
Is she gone?

Morning comes the sunrise and I'm driven to my bed
I see that it is empty and there's devils in my head
I embrace the many-colored beast
I grow weary of the torment
Can there be no peace?
And I find myself just wishin'
That my life would simply cease.

Don McLean

AMERICAN PIE

The intrepid explorer may be able to survey a relatively intact history of rock 'n' roll mapped onto Don McLean's "American Pie," one of the biggest hits of 1971, and one of the longest pop songs ever (eight and one-half minutes). The lyric hinges on a doomy conceit —"the day the music died"—which seems to relate the death of rock's innocence to the death of Buddy Holly, whose classic "That'll Be the Day" is echoed in McLean's elegiac chorus. Of course, McLean is using rock as an American symbol in the broadest sense, although one may detect metaphoric references to just about every rocker—from Elvis ("the king") to Dylan ("the jester") to The Beatles ("the sergeants") to Mick Jagger ("Jack Flash")—who helped shape the consciousness of the '60s and, along with events, brought about the end of our collective childhood. Still, the poetic power of the lyric lies not in its particulars so much as in its sweeping sense of a culture confronting emptiness—"Drove my Chevy to the levee/ But the levee was dry"—where so much promise had been.

AMERICAN PIE

A long long time ago
I can still remember how that music
Used to make me smile.
And I knew if I had my chance
That I could make those people dance
And maybe they'd be happy for a while.
But February made me shiver
With every paper I'd deliver.
Bad news on the doorstep,
I couldn't take one more step.
I can't remember if I cried
When I read about his widowed bride,
But something touched me deep inside
The day the music died.

So Bye Bye Miss American Pie,
Drove my Chevy to the levee
But the levee was dry.
Them good old boys were drinkin' whisky and rye
Singin', This'll be the day that I die,
This'll be the day that I die.

Did you write the book of love?
And do you have faith in God above
If the bible tells you so?
And do you believe in rock and roll?
Can music save your mortal soul?
And can you teach me how to dance real slow?
Well I know that you're in love with him
'Cause I saw you dancing in the gym.
You both kicked off your shoes,
Man I dig those rhythm and blues.
I was a lonely teenage broncin' buck
With a pink carnation and a pickup truck,
But I knew I was out of luck
The day the music died.

I was singin', Bye Bye Miss American Pie
Drove my Chevy to the levee
But the levee was dry.
Them good old boys were drinkin' whisky and rye,
Singin', This'll be the day that I die,
This'll be the day that I die.

Now for ten years we've been on our own
And moss grows fat on a rolling stone
But that's not how it used to be.
When the jester sang for the king and queen
In a coat he'd borrowed from James Dean
And a voice that came from you and me.
Oh and while the king was looking down,
The jester stole his thorny crown.
The courtroom was adjourned,
No verdict was returned.
And while Lennon read a book of Marx,
The quartet practiced in the park,
And we sang dirges in the dark
The day the music died.

We were singin', Bye Bye Miss American Pie
Drove my Chevy to the levee
But the levee was dry.
Them good old boys were drinkin' whiskey and rye,
Singin', This'll be the day that I die,
This'll be the day that I die.

Helter skelter in a summer swelter
The birds flew off with a fallout shelter,
Eight miles high and fallin' fast.
It landed foul on the grass,
The players tried for a forward pass,
With the jester on the sidelines in a cast.
Now the halftime air was sweet perfume
While the sergeants played a marching tune.
We all got up to dance
Oh but we never got the chance.
'Cause the players tried to take the field,
The marching band refused to yield.
Do you recall what was revealed
The day the music died?

We started singin',
Bye Bye Miss American Pie,
Drove my Chevy to the levee
But the levee was dry.
Them good old boys were drinkin' whiskey and rye,
Singin', This'll be the day that I die,
This'll be the day that I die.

Oh and there we were all in one place,
A generation lost in space

With no time left to start again.
So c'mon Jack be nimble, Jack be quick,
Jack Flash sat on a candlestick
'Cause fire is the devil's only friend.
And as I watched him on the stage
My hands were clenched in fists of rage.
No angel born in hell
Could break that satan's spell.
And as the flames climbed high into the night
To light the sacrificial right,
I saw satan laughing with delight
The day the music died.

He was singin', Bye Bye Miss American Pie
Drove my Chevy to the levee
But the levee was dry.
Them good old boys were drinkin' whiskey and rye,
Singin' This'll be the day that I die,
This'll be the day that I die.

I met a girl who sang the blues
And I asked her for some happy news.
She just smiled and turned away.
I went down to the sacred store
Where I'd heard the music years before,
But the man there said the music wouldn't play.
And in the streets the children screamed,
The lovers cried and the poets dreamed
But not a word was spoken,
The churchbells all were broken.
And the three men I admire most,
The Father, Son and Holy Ghost,
They caught the last train for the coast
The day the music died.

And they were singin',
Bye Bye Miss American Pie,
Drove my Chevy to the levee
But the levee was dry.
Them good old boys were drinkin' whiskey and rye,
Singin' this'll be the day that I die.

Janis Ian

SOCIETY'S CHILD

If she hadn't been a child of '60s society, Janis Ian would probably have emerged as a prodigy of classical music, but the combination of her precocious talent and the cultural forces of the day led her more naturally to a fusion of folk, jazz, and rock. At only fifteen, this shy New Yorker set the 1967 pop world on its ear with an extraordinary song, "Society's Child." About a white girl and a black boy whose young love can't elude the harsh social realities, this lyric, with its haunting refrain—"I can't see you anymore, baby"—touched the nerve of liberal America's racial hypocrisy. Beyond that, it introduced a new poetic voice, a voice capable of isolating a range of emotional complexity from a stark yet highly refined urban viewpoint.

SOCIETY'S CHILD (BABY I'VE BEEN THINKING)

Come to my door, baby.
Face is clean and shining black as night.
My mother went to answer your note
That you wrote so fine.
Now I can understand your tears and your shame,
She called you "boy" instead of your name.
When she wouldn't let you inside,
When she turned and said, "But honey,
He's not our kind."

She says I can't see you anymore, baby,
Can't see you anymore.

Walk me down to school, baby.
Everybody's acting deaf and blind,
Until they turn and say,
"Why don't you stick to your own kind?"
My teachers all laugh,
Their smirking stares
Cutting deep down in our affairs.
Preachers of equality,
If they believe it then why won't
They just let us be?

They say I can't see you anymore, baby,
Can't see you anymore.

One of these days I'm gonna stop my listening,
Gonna raise my head up high.
One of these days I'm gonna raise my glistening
Wings and fly.
But that day will have to wait for a while.
Baby I'm only society's child.
When we're older things may change.
But for now this is the way they must remain.

I say I can't see you anymore, baby,
Can't see you anymore.
No, I don't want to see you anymore, baby.

Robert Hunter and The Grateful Dead

UNCLE JOHN'S BAND

Of all the bands representing San Francisco's Bay Area rock scene, only The Grateful Dead has survived more or less intact, bridging the gap between the most cryptic, convoluted acid-rock of the '60s and the rock-for-rock's-sake of the '70s. Renowned mainly for the seasoned flow, eclectic tangents, and eccentric, counter-cultural cast of their instrumental jams, the Dead have also given us lyrics—most of them from the pen of non-performer Robert Hunter—which stand with the best in rock. Hunter's "Uncle John's Band," for example, from the Dead's 1970 album *Workingman's Dead* —in which they swung to soft, acoustic, high-harmony rock—is a lyric that extends the '60s notion of music as the glue of communal enterprise, but with a sense of beginnings, of lessons learned, and of cautious optimism ("when life looks like Easy Street there is danger at your door").

The imagery is simple but evocative, from the hint of folksy self-determination that echoes James Dickey's poetry ("It's a buck-dancer's choice my friend"), to the crisp observation of society's old, rigid, warlike guard ("Their walls are built of cannonballs;/ Their motto is: 'Don't tread on me' "). Without burning bridges, this lyric seems to cross the border from one decade to the next.

UNCLE JOHN'S BAND

Well, the first days are the hardest days;
Don't you worry any more,
'Cause when life looks like Easy Street,
There is danger at your door.
Think this through with me;
Let me know your mind.
Wo—oh, what I want to know is,
Are you kind?

It's a buckdancer's choice my friend;
Better take my advice.
You know all the rules by now
And the fire from the ice
Will you come with me?
Won't you come with me?
Wo—oh, what I want to know:
Will you come with me?

God damn, well I declare,
Have you seen the like?
Their walls are built of cannonballs;
Their motto is:
"Don't tread on me."
Come hear Uncle John's Band
Playing to the tide.
Come with me or go alone,
He's come to take his children home.

It's the same story the crow told me,
It's the only one he knows.
Like the morning sun you come and
Like the wind you go.
Ain't no time to hate,
Barely time to wait.
Wo—oh, what I want to know:
Where does the time go?

I live in a silver mine
And I call it Beggar's Tomb.
I got me a violin and I
Beg you call the tune.
Anybody's choice, I can hear your voice.

Wo—oh, what I want to know:
How does the song go?

Come hear Uncle John's Band
By the riverside.
Got some things to talk about
Here beside the rising tide.
Come hear Uncle John's Band
Playing to the tide.
Come on along or go alone,
He's come to take his children home.

BOX OF RAIN

The *American Beauty* album closely followed *Workingman's Dead* in 1970, but with a more pronounced country-pop feel that seemed to place The Grateful Dead squarely in the middle of the road. Although more accessible to the masses than ever before, Robert Hunter's lyrics had compromised none of their poetic character, their flair for an abstract image smoothly turned. "Box of Rain" is a perfect example of this—a lyric that confronts the evanescence of our selves, our days, our dreams ("In and out the window like a moth/ Before a flame") and implies the value of our attachments despite their impermanence ("just a box of rain,/ Or a ribbon for your hair/ Such a long long time to be gone/ And a short time to be there"). With its breezy expressions of willing sacrifice, of instinct above experience ("feel your way, feel your way like the day before"), it encourages our faith in the larger forces without preaching or presuming ("just a box of rain;/ I don't know who put it there/ believe it if you need it/ or leave it if you dare") and seems to signal the end of all strident '60s rhetoric.

BOX OF RAIN

Look out of any window,
Any morning, any evening,
Any day.
Maybe the sun is shining, birds are winging,
No rain is falling from
A heavy sky.
What do you want me to do,
To do for you,
To see you through?
For this is all a dream we dreamed
One afternoon long ago.

Walk out of any doorway,
Feel your way, feel your way
Like the day before.
Maybe you'll find direction
Around some corner where it's been
Waiting to meet you.
What do you want me to do,
To watch for you while you're sleeping?
Then please don't be surprised when you find
Me dreaming too.

Look into any eyes
You find by you;
You can see clear to another day.
Maybe been seen before,
Through other eyes on other days
While going home.
What do you want me to do,
To do for you,
To see you through?
It's all a dream we dreamed
One afternoon long ago.

Walk into splintered sunlight,
Inch your way through dead dreams
To another land.
Maybe you're tired and broken,
Your tongue is twisted
With words half-spoken
And thoughts unclear.

What do you want me to do,
To do for you, to see you through?

A box of rain will ease the pain
And love will see you through.
Just a box of rain, wind and water.
Believe it if you need it,
If you don't just pass it on.
Sun and shower, wind and rain,
In and out the window like a moth
Before a flame.

And it's just a box of rain;
I don't know who put it there;
Believe it if you need it
Or leave it if you dare,
And it's just a box of rain,
Or a ribbon for your hair;
Such a long long time to be gone
And a short time to be there.

John Barlow

CASSIDY

While Robert Hunter has penned most of The Grateful Dead's words, another close friend of the band, John Barlow, has contributed a number of first-rate lyrics to the Dead's repertoire. One of his best, "Cassidy," surfaced in 1972, when leading Deadmen Jerry Garcia, Bob Weir, and Mickey Hart had begun to branch out with a series of marginally successful solo albums. The most listenable and enduring of these is Weir's album *Ace,* and "Cassidy" is probably its strongest track. Barlow's abstract yet convincingly personal depiction of arrival, intimacy, and continuity amidst death, distance, and leave-taking is studded with such vivid imagery and propelled by such a brisk rhythm ("quick beats in an icy heart") that it sings almost as vibrantly on paper as it does through Weir's perfect melody.

CASSIDY

I have seen where the wolf has slept
By the silver stream.
I can tell by the mark he left
You were in his dream.
Ah, child of countless trees.
Ah, child of boundless seas.
What you are, what you're meant to be
Speaks his name, though you're born to me,
Born to me, Cassidy.

Lost now in the country miles
With his Cadillac.
I can tell by the way you smile,
He is rolling back.
Come, wash the night-time clean.
Come, grow the scorched ground green.
Blow the horn, tap the tambourine.
Close the gap of dark years in between
You and me, Cassidy.

Quick beats in an icy heart.
Catch-colt draws a coffin-cart.
There he goes, here she starts.
I hear her cry.
Flight of the seabirds,
Scattered like lost words,
Wheel to the storm and fly.

Faring thee well now, let your life proceed
By its own design.
Nothing to tell, let the words be yours,
I am done with mine.

Jim Morrison and The Doors

THE END

Jim Morrison's death in 1971 completed the American trinity of '60s rock martyrs that began with Jimi Hendrix's death in 1969 and took Janis Joplin the following year. While each of them had lived dangerously on the edges of life and art, only Morrison seemed to have hinted at his end with the elemental Freudian symbolism of his death-wish lyrics. As lead singer and figurehead of The Doors, Morrison rose to heights of mystique in the late '60s and described himself early on, with typical sardonic clarity, as an "erotic politician."

There's no better example of his erotic politics than "The End," the long vatic finale of The Doors's 1967 debut album. With its intimations of apocalypse ("of everything that stands,/ The end"), its shamanistic invocation of some reptilian id ("Ride the snake/ To the lake"), its Oedipal climax ("Father . . . I want to kill you"), this lyric wrenched pop music from the paisley whimsicalities of acid-rock and focused on the murky depths of the subconscious; it provoked a confrontation between music's outward celebration and our inner evils, hidden demons, buried obsessions. Francis Ford Coppola chose the song as the key theme of his 1979 film, *Apocalypse Now,* and indeed, more than a decade after its initial appearance, this lyric still strikes at the very heart of darkness.

THE END

This is the end,
Beautiful friend,
This is the end,
My only friend,
The end of our elaborate plans,
The end of everything that stands,
The end. No safety or surprise,
The end. I'll never look into your eyes
Again.

Can you picture what will be,
So limitless and free,
Desperately in need of some stranger's hand
In a desperate land.
Lost in a Roman wilderness of pain
And all the children are insane.
All the children are insane;
Waiting for the summer rain.

There's danger on the edge of town,
Ride the king's highway.
Weird scenes inside the gold mine;
Ride the king's highway west, baby.
Ride the snake
To the lake,
The ancient lake.
The snake is long,
Seven miles;
Ride the snake,
He's old and his skin is cold.

The West is the best.
The West is the best.
Get here and we'll do the rest.
The blue bus is calling us.
Driver, where you taking us?

The killer awoke before dawn,
He put his boots on,
He took a face from the ancient gallery,
And he walked on down the hall.
He went to the room where his sister lived,

And then he paid a visit to his brother,
And then he walked on down the hall.
And he came to a door.
And he looked inside.

"Father?"
"Yes, son?"
"I want to kill you."
"Mother, I want to . . ."

Come on baby, take a chance with us,
And meet me by the back of the blue bus.

This is the end,
Beautiful friend.
This is the end,
My only friend, the end.
It hurts to set you free
But you'll never follow me.
The end of laughter and soft lies,
The end of nights we tried to die.
This is the end.

Laura Nyro

STONED SOUL PICNIC

It's a tribute to Laura Nyro's passion and originality that her style still exerts a major influence on emerging female rock artists, while she herself has lived virtually in retirement since her own emergence in the mid-'60s. Except for occasional recording and sporadic touring, this reclusive New Yorker has remained incompatible with the "star-maker machinery" (Joni Mitchell's phrase) by which pop artists produce, are produced, and for better and worse, sustained. What's more, this machinery has never found anyone to stand in for Laura Nyro, often described as the "white soul diva" who transformed the melting-pot spontaneity of New York street-sing—in its multicolored black, white, and Hispanic intensity—into a gospel that connected with the fey communalism of the hippie flower-power movement.

From the start, her ability to pen hit songs—"And When I Die" for "Blood, Sweat and Tears," "Stoney End" for Barbra Streisand, two for the Fifth Dimension—obscured her poetry from its most personal associations, which were asserted on her second album, *Eli and the 13th Confession* (1968). From that collection, "Stoned Soul Picnic" stands as the quintessential Laura Nyro lyric—an open invitation to some hippie-era celebration where all the promise of a new age seems to be checking in on "trains of music . . . trains of trust/ trains of golden dust." This is a poem of the purest sound and spirit; the "stoned soul" celebrants "surry down" to bask in "time and wine/ red yellow honey/ sassafrass and moonshine," and a boundless faith in love, "the Lord and the lightnin'," is the most intoxicating drug around.

STONED SOUL PICNIC

Can you surry
Can you picnic?
Can you surry
Can you picnic?
Surry down
To a stoned soul picnic
Surry down
To a stoned soul picnic
There'll be lots of time and wine
Red yellow honey
Sassafras and moonshine
Red yellow honey sassafras and moonshine
Stoned soul.

Surry down
To a stoned soul picnic
Surry down
To a stoned soul picnic
Rain and sun come in akin
And from the sky come the Lord
And the lightnin
And from the sky come the Lord and the lightnin
Stoned soul.

Surry surry surry surry
There'll be trains of blossoms
There'll be trains of music
There'll be trains of trust
Trains of golden dust
Come along and surry on sweet trains of thought
Surry on down
Can you surry?

Surry down
To a stoned soul picnic
Surry down
To a stoned soul picnic
There'll be lots of time and wine
Red yellow honey
Sassafras and moonshine
Red yellow honey
Sassafras and moonshine

Red yellow honey
Sassafras
And moonshine moonshine
Stoned soul.

Joni Mitchell

SISOTOWBELL LANE

One could rate Joni Mitchell as Bob Dylan's counterpart among folk-rock poets, although not by virtue of similarity. Dylan's lyric style has been characterized by an elusive personal quality and by a somewhat less disciplined brand of wordsmithing. Joni Mitchell's has been consistently more confessional and more precisely calibrated in its imagery. And where Dylan's music has ranged greatly —from folk-protest to rock-gospel and just about every permutation in between—Joni Mitchell has evolved less radically through rock, pop, and jazz currents. With increasing sophistication, she's kept on sketching a confined inner landscape of romantic anxiety, wherein the piercing sensitivity of an artistic temperament is frequently in conflict with the roles of celebrity, lady, lover.

Perhaps the main parallel that could be drawn between Joni Mitchell and Bob Dylan is that both rose to prominence mainly through other artists' interpretations of their songs. In the mid-'60s, for example, such folksingers as Tom Rush, Judy Collins, Dave Van Ronk, and Buffy Sainte-Marie were generating more pop interest with Joni Mitchell material—mainly "Urge for Going" and "Clouds (Both Sides Now)"—than with anything else in their repertoires. Anonymously at first, these early songs defined the graceful intensity of introspection that had been forged in Joni Mitchell's native Alberta, at the foot of the Canadian Rockies, and refined in the folk clubs of Toronto and New York. Her self-titled debut album of 1968 was produced by David Crosby, although the master tapes were accidentally damaged and had to be restored by a process that inevitably muted the high notes. As a result, the album sounds, as Joni Mitchell once described it to Philadelphia folklorist Gene Shay, "like we recorded it under a bell jar." Artistically, this fateful muting only succeeded in suggesting the fragile sensibility of a new poetic heroine, one whose lyrics echoed the finely tuned feminine anguish and exaltation of Sylvia Plath.

"A poet can sing/ Sometimes we try/ Yes we always try" is Joni Mitchell's affirmation in "Sisotowbell Lane," one of her first album's most evocative lyrics. As she revealed in an early interview, the name "Sisotowbell" is actually an acronym of blind romantic optimism ("Somehow in Spite of Trouble Ours Will Be Ever Lasting Love") although the lyric is more a vision of domestic tranquillity, idealized on one hand yet made tangible by such lines as "Eating muffin buns and berries/ By the steamy kitchen window." These clues suggest that the aging dreamer's best refuge is only the familiar home of the child.

SISOTOWBELL LANE

Sisotowbell Lane
Noah is fixing the pump in the rain
He brings us no shame
We always knew that he always knew
Up over the hill
Jovial neighbors come down when they will
With stories to tell
Sometimes they do
Yes sometimes we do
We have a rocking chair
Each of us rocks his share
Eating muffin buns and berries
By the steamy kitchen window
Sometimes we do
Our tongues turn blue

Sisotowbell Lane
Anywhere else now would seem very strange
The seasons are changing
Everyday in everyway
Sometimes it is spring
Sometimes it is not anything
A poet can sing
Sometimes we try
Yes we always try
We have a rocking chair
Somedays we rock and stare
At the woodlands and the grasslands and
The badlands 'cross the river
Sometimes we do
We like the view

Sisotowbell Lane
Go to the city you'll come back again
To wade through the grain
You always do
Yes we always do
Come back to the stars
Sweet well water and pickling jars
We'll lend you the car
We always do
Yes sometimes we do

We have a rocking chair
Someone is always there
Rocking rhythms while they're waiting
With the candle in the window
Sometimes we do
We wait for you

A CASE OF YOU

Joni Mitchell's fourth album, *Blue* (1971), marked her transition from folkie flower-child, song-painting a fanciful vision of '60s introspection, to a chronicler of adult dilemma and shattered illusion. With this album, the childlike wonder of Joni Mitchell's previous material had given way not only to the pervasive blue mood of the title but to a sort of lyric conversationalism that suggests the penetrating inner dialogue and conflicting immediacy of a complex psyche. At last liberated from the rather formal metric schemes of her early lyrics, the Joni Mitchell of *Blue* had evolved the ultimate poetic voice for her most mature self-expression.

"A Case of You," the most affirmative of the love lyrics on *Blue,* beautifully illustrates this unique blend of conversation, confession, and poetic clueing. For example, the shift in emotional emphasis, from the depressed dismissiveness of "If you want me I'll be in the bar," to the vulnerable revelation of a later line ("I drew a map of Canada/ . . . With your face sketched on it twice"), to the exalted avowal of the chorus, suggests the ambivalent dimension of a difficult relationship. The refrain—"in my blood like holy wine/ . . . so bitter and so sweet/ Oh I could drink a case of you, darling/ And I would still be on my feet"—is blatantly sexual on one hand, while on the other it invokes the symbolism of trans-substantiation, of romantic love as holy nourishment. This kind of intensity and clarity—the soul in conflict, but not confused—informs much of Joni Mitchell's best work, and though her later lyrics reveal a sadder-but-wiser swallowing of the bitter pill, the sense of spiritual quest, of faith at least in the *feeling,* remains.

A CASE OF YOU

Just before our love got lost you said,
"I am as constant as a northern star."
And I said, "Constantly in the darkness
Where's that at?
If you want me I'll be in the bar."
On the back of a cartoon coaster
In the blue T.V. screen light
I drew a map of Canada
Oh, Canada
With your face sketched on it twice.
Oh, you are in my blood like holy wine
You taste so bitter and so sweet
Oh, I could drink a case of you, darling
And I would still be on my feet
I would still be on my feet.

Oh, I am a lonely painter
I live in a box of paints
I'm frightened by the devil
And I'm drawn to those ones that ain't afraid.
I remember that time you told me, you said,
"Love is touching souls."
Well surely you touched mine
'Cause part of you pours out of me
In these lines from time to time.
Oh, you're in my blood like holy wine
You taste so bitter and so sweet
Oh, I could drink a case of you, darling
And I would still be on my feet
I would still be on my feet.

I met a woman
She had a mouth like yours
She knew your lies
She knew your devils and your deeds
And she said, "Go to him, stay with him
If you can
But be prepared to bleed."
But you are in my blood

You're my holy wine
You taste so bitter and so sweet
Oh, I could drink a case of you, darling
And I would still be on my feet
I would still be on my feet.

AMELIA

As Joni Mitchell began to navigate the popular mainstream of the 1970s, her music spoke to its growing audience with less acoustic-folk purity and more experimentalism. It mixed her guitar, piano, and pristine soprano with the mellow-rock accompaniment of Los Angeles sessionmen and a range of jazz-pop voicings and orchestrations. The result was an often icy North American fusion, a model of pop sophistication with a layered aural tension to match the increasing complexity and troubled social commentary of the lyrics. This development peaked with the 1975 album, *The Hissing of Summer Lawns.* The following year, Joni Mitchell broke from its attenuations with *Hejira,* the album that restored her to her acoustic-folk roots, but also built a bridge—subtly, with the original, articulate help of electric bassist Jaco Pastorius—to the jazz vanguard. The lyrics reflect this streamlining of sound and purpose with their mingling of mature self-awareness and a fully stylized symbology of the holy romantic quest (the album's title refers to the prophet Mohammed's flight from Mecca to Medina).

"Amelia," for example, invokes the womanly symbol, spirit, style, and ultimately, the enigma of aviatrix Amelia Earhart. Here, Joni Mitchell is obviously identifying with a heroine, but beyond that she is looking back on the symbols and style of her own legend, and at how her artist's perfectionism has impinged on imperfect life. With its reference to the "Cactus Tree Motel," an echo from her first album ("and her heart is full and hollow/ like a cactus tree/ while she's so busy bein' free,") and to "Clouds (Both Sides Now)" ("I've spent my whole life in clouds at icy altitudes"), "Amelia" is a song about selfish freedom and impossible aspirations catching up with us; about "Icarus ascending/ On beautiful foolish arms," only to nose-dive, heavy with "dreams and false alarms."

AMELIA

I was driving across the burning desert
When I spotted six jet planes
Leaving six white vapor trails across the bleak terrain
It was the hexagram of the heavens
It was the strings of my guitar
Amelia, it was just a false alarm.

The drone of flying engines
Is a song so wild and blue
It scrambles time and seasons if it gets thru to you
Then your life becomes a travelogue
Of picture-post-card-charms
Amelia, it was a false alarm.

People will tell you where they've gone
They'll tell you where to go
But till you get there yourself you never really know
Where some have found their paradise
Others just come to harm
Amelia, it was just a false alarm.

I wish that he were here tonight
It's so hard to obey
His sad request of me to stay away
So this is how I hide the hurt
As the road leads cursed and charmed
I tell Amelia it was just a false alarm.

A ghost of aviation
She was swallowed by the sky
Or by the sea, like me she had a dream to fly
Like Icarus ascending
On beautiful foolish arms
Amelia, it was just a false alarm.

Maybe I've never really loved
I guess that is the truth
I've spent my whole life in clouds at icy altitudes
And looking down on everything
I crashed into his arms
Amelia, it was just a false alarm.

I pulled into the Cactus Tree Motel
To shower off the dust
And I slept on the strange pillows of my wanderlust
I dreamed of 747's
Over geometric farms
Dreams, Amelia, dreams and false alarms.

FURRY SINGS THE BLUES

This lyric, also from *Hejira,* seems to prefigure Joni Mitchell's immersion in the waters of black jazz, which would come during her 1978–79 collaboration with dying jazz giant Charles Mingus. In this lyric, tribute is paid to another withering giant of black music, Memphis bluesman Furry Lewis. Stripped of the neurasthenic self-absorption that pervades the bulk of Joni Mitchell's most adult lyrics, "Furry Sings the Blues" affords the painterly poetic distance of her youthful masterworks as well as a deft conversational quality. The elegiac power of this lyric is achieved metaphorically, but there's no metaphoric stretching—only pure poetic justice—in its journalistic observations. They equate the physical decay of a spirited old man with that of his urban turf, suggesting how Furry and old Beale Street reflect and define each other—"Pawn shops glitter like gold tooth caps"—and haunt us, accuse us, in their splendid squalor.

FURRY SINGS THE BLUES

Old Beale Street is coming down
Sweenies' Snack Bar, boarded up now
And Egles The Tailor and the shine boy's gone
Faded out with ragtime blues
Handy's cast in bronze
And he's standing in a little park
With his trumpet in his hand
Like he's listening back to the good old bands
And the click of high-heeled shoes
Old Furry sings the blues
Propped up in his bed
With his dentures and his leg removed
And Ginny's there
For her kindness and Furry's beer
She's the old man's angel overseer.

Pawn shops glitter like gold tooth caps
In the grey decay
They chew the last few dollars off old Beale Street's carcass
Carrion and mercy
Blue and silver sparkling drums
Cheap guitars, eye shades and guns
Aimed at the hot blood of being no one
Down and out in Memphis Tennessee
Old Furry sings the blues
You bring him smoke and drink and he'll play for you
It's mostly muttering now and sideshow spiel
But there was one song he played
I could really feel.

There's a double bill murder at the New Daisy
The old girl's silent across the street
She's silent-waiting for the wreckers' beat
Silent-staring at her stolen name
Diamond boys and satin dolls
Bourbon laughter-ghosts-history falls
To parking lots and shopping malls
As they tear down old Beale Street
Old Furry sings the blues
He points a bony finger at you and says,
"I don't like you"
Everybody laughs as if it's the old man's standard joke

But it's true
We're only welcome for our drink and smoke.

W.C. Handy I'm rich and I'm fey
And I'm not familiar with what you played
But I get such strong impressions of your heyday
Looking up and down old Beale Street
Ghosts of the darktown society
Come right out of the bricks at me
Like it's a Saturday night
They're in their finery
Dancing it up and making deals
Furry sings the blues
Why should I expect that old guy to give it to me true
Fallin' to hard luck
And time and other thieves
While our limo is shining on his shanty street
Old Furry sings the blues.

Robbie Robertson and The Band

THE WEIGHT

The Band made rock 'n' roll sound as if it had been around since the mid-1800s and still hadn't strayed too far from the prairie. Indeed, their emergence and success in the late 1960s went against the grain of an acid-rock sound that had grown too narcissistic. Where most of the day's music was obsessed with star-tripping, innovation, and the shattering of old values, The Band upheld the timeless musical tradition and fundamental morality bred in heartland America, reflected in its blues, rags, hollers, hymns, laments, and refracted by their unmistakable core of country-flavored rock. Without flashy effect or egocentricity—three of the five shared lead vocal chores, while guitarist Robbie Robertson, who wrote most of the material, barely sang at all—The Band suggested contentment with American myth, archetype, and tradition, and their songs amounted to dramatic meditations on the Old West, the Sherman-trod South, the mountain life. Throughout, as critic Greil Marcus contends, there ran a thread of longing, the longing of the outsider, for all but one of The Band—drummer Levon Helm, an Arkansas native—had come from Canada. As outsiders retelling and fantasizing the rustic side of America's story, they injected a peculiar tension, respect, and playfulness.

They began as Levon and the Hawks, loyal men behind Canada's "wildman" rocker, Ronnie Hawkins, who had recruited them from high school and mastered them through the funkiest, brawlingest, redneck-rural joints in America. Fatefully, Bob Dylan called upon the Hawks to back his Hollywood Bowl concert of the 1965 summer, and they proved to be his greatest backers, onstage and in the recording studio. They even "retired" with him to Woodstock, following his 1966 motorcycle accident. There, The Band's sober fundamentalism seemed to rub off on Dylan, and Dylan's lyric ambiguity rubbed off on songwriter Robertson.

The shining example of this Dylanized Band is Robertson's "The Weight," from The Band's 1968 debut album, *Music from Big Pink.* In discussing the song, Robertson has noted, "I was kind of hung up on Luis Buñuel, the Spanish film maker. He's made a few films on saints and it just doesn't work in this world, being a saint." The lyric's theme seems to be one of redemption through faith—"I pulled into Nazareth,/ . . . feelin' 'bout half past dead"—although the mood is mainly secular. And yet the verses brim with clues suggesting "no room at the inn" ("He just grinned, shook my hand,/ 'No' was all he said"), the choice between peace and war, good and evil. On the edge where parable borders absurdity, "The Weight" inhabits an oddly touchable time and space, where people speak a mystery tongue we somehow understand only too well.

THE WEIGHT

I pulled into Nazareth,
I was feelin' 'bout half past dead.
I just needed some place where I could lay my head.
Hey mister can you tell me where a man might find a bed?
He just grinned, shook my hand,
"No" was all he said.

Take a load off, Annie.
Take a load for free.
Take a load off, Annie.
And you put the load right on me.

I picked up my bag,
I went looking for a place to hide.
Then I saw Carmen and the Devil walking side by side.
I said "Hey, Carmen, c'mon let's go downtown."
She said, "I gotta go but my friend is still around."

Take a load off, Annie.
Take a load for free.
Take a load off, Annie.
And you put the load right on me.

Go down to Miss Moses,
There's nothing you can say.
It's just old Luke and Luke's waitin' on the Judgement Day.
Well Luke my friend,
What about young Anna Lee?
He said, "Do me a favor, son,
Won't you stay and keep Anna Lee company?"

Take a load off, Annie.
Take a load for free.
Take a load off, Annie.
And you put the load right on me.

Crazy Chester followed me
And he caught me in the bog.
He said, "I will fix your rack
If you'll take Jack my dog."
I said "Wait a minute Chester,
Y'know I'm a peaceful man."

He said, "That's okay, boy,
Won't you feed me when you can?"

Take a load off, Annie.
Take a load for free.
Take a load off, Annie.
And you put the load right on me.

Engine Cannonball now to take me down the line.
My back is sinkin' low and I do believe it's time
To get back to Miss Fanny,
You know she's the only one
Who sent me here with her regards for everyone.

Take a load off, Annie.
Take a load for free.
Take a load off, Annie.
And you put the load right on me.

THE NIGHT THEY DROVE OLE DIXIE DOWN

At their most visionary and journalistic, Robbie Robertson's songs for The Band conveyed mythic American circumstance with the earthy realism and sepia-toned artistry of a Brady daguerreotype. And no lyric was better suited to this aural task than "The Night They Drove Ole Dixie Down," from The Band's self-titled second album of 1969. It's an apocalyptic vision of the last days of the Civil War from the viewpoint of a dispossessed Southern farmer whose heartbreak in defeat is tempered by a gritty fatalism and a transcendent sense of belonging to the land ("I swear by the mud below my feet"). Bells toll in the chorus, as does wordless, mournful emotion when the conquered sing, "na na na na na na." These "na na's," which usually serve to denote rock 'n' roll's mindless, sing--songy sense of fun, were recast by the lyric's sad historical setting and transformed into a profound hymn of inexpressible loss. Above all, the incidental details of the farmer's heartfelt testimony—"I served on the Danville train . . . By May the tenth, Richmond had fell"—are what lend this lyric such humanity and haunted immediacy.

THE NIGHT THEY DROVE OLE DIXIE DOWN

Virgil Cain is the name
And I served on the Danville train
'Til Stoneman's cavalry came
And tore up the tracks again.
In the winter of '65, we were hungry,
Just barely alive.
By May the tenth, Richmond had fell,
It took time, I remember oh so well.

The night they drove ole Dixie down,
And the bells were ringin',
The night they drove ole Dixie down,
And all the people were singin', they went
"Na Na Na Na Na Na,
Na Na Na Na, Na Na Na Na . . ."

Back with my wife in Tennessee,
When one day she called to me,
"Virgil, quick come see,
There go the Robert E. Lee."
Now I don't mind choppin' wood,
And I don't care if the money's no good.
You take what you need and you leave the rest,
But they should never have taken the very best.

The night they drove ole Dixie down,
The bells were ringin',
The night they drove ole Dixie down,
All the people were singin', they went
"Na Na Na Na Na Na, Na Na Na Na,
Na Na Na Na . . ."

Like my father before me, I will work the land.
And like my brother below me, who took a rebel stand,
He was just eighteen, proud and brave,
But a Yankee laid him in his grave.
I swear by the mud below my feet,
You can't raise a king back up when he's in defeat.

The night they drove ole Dixie down,
The bells were ringin',

The night they drove ole Dixie down,
And all the people were singin', they went
"Na Na Na Na Na Na, Na Na Na Na,
Na Na Na Na . . ."

Jesse Winchester

BILOXI

America's great singer-songwriter in exile, Jesse Winchester fled to Canada in 1967 rather than face induction in a Vietnam-bound army. A native of Shreveport, Lousiana, Winchester—a quiet man of plain style—identified in his music with the faded gentility and lazy life-rhythm of the Old South. At the same time, his roots took well in Canadian soil, and his absorbancy led to a North American folk sound rich in cross-cultural influence and outlook. When President Carter's amnesty for Vietnam draft evaders permitted his return in 1977, Winchester toured briefly for the American fans he had been cultivating since The Band's Robbie Robertson had discovered and recorded him in 1970, but by then Winchester had become too much a Canadian to call America his home.

Ironically, none of Winchester's lyrics protest the war he had refused to abet; instead, they reflect the stoic faith and bittersweet longings of a man cut off from his native soil, but very much alive to his native past. "Biloxi," from Winchester's 1970 debut album, evokes a time and place made holy by the singer's expression of simple pleasure profoundly recalled. The imagery mingles macrocosm and microcosm—"Stars can see Biloxi . . . and the sun will set from off toward New Orleans"—as if to chart a walk in the sand with a map of heaven.

BILOXI

Down around Biloxi,
Pretty girls are swimming in the sea.
Oh they look like sisters in the ocean,
The boy will fill his pail with salted water,
And the storms will blow from off toward New Orleans.

The sun shines on Biloxi,
The air is filled with vapors from the sea.
And the boy will dig a pool beside the ocean,
He sees creatures from a dream on the water,
And the sun will set from off toward New Orleans.

Stars can see Biloxi,
The stars can find their faces in the sea.
And we are walking in the evening by the ocean,
We are splashing naked in the water,
And the sky is red from off toward New Orleans.

YANKEE LADY

The sensual clues of time and place are what give Jesse Winchester's "Yankee Lady" such resonance. Also from Winchester's 1970 debut album, the lyric charts the course of a season's idyll with an older woman and an initiation into manhood. Here, the simple traditional pleasures of rustic domesticity are viewed with reverence ("apple cider and homemade bread/ To make a man say grace") while the joys of awakening sexuality are beatifically recalled ("And I smile like the sun to think of the lovin'/ That we did"). Winchester invests this rich memory with a fully integrated poetry of passage, from wandering youth to hearth-loving and ultimately restless manhood, from season to season, from time savored to time consumed ("An autumn walk on a country road/ And a million flaming trees"), while the Yankee lady of the song stands for all the comforting constancy of a land left behind.

YANKEE LADY

I lived with the decent folk in the hills of old Vermont,
Where what you do all day depends on what you want.
And I took up with a woman there
Though I was still a kid,
And I smile like the sun to think of the lovin'
That we did.
She rose each morning and went to work
And she kept me with her pay.
I was making love all night
And playing guitar all day.
And I got me apple cider and homemade bread
To make a man say grace,
And clean linens on my bed
And a warm-feet fireplace.

Yankee lady so good to me,
Yankee lady just a memory.
Yankee lady so good to me,
Your memory, that's enough for me.

An autumn walk on a country road
And a million flaming trees.
I was feeling uneasy because there was
Winter in the breeze.
And she said, "Oh Jesse, look over there,
The birds are southward bound.
Oh Jesse, I'm so afraid
To lose the love that we found."

Yankee lady so good to me,
Yankee lady just a memory.
Yankee lady so good to me,
Your memory, that's enough for me.

I don't know what called to me
But I know that I had to go.
And I left that Vermont town with a lift to Mexico.
And now when I see myself
As a stranger by my birth,
The Yankee lady's memory reminds me of my worth.

Yankee lady so good to me,
Yankee lady just a memory.
Yankee lady so good to me,
Your memory, that's enough for me.

Randy Newman

I THINK IT'S GOING TO RAIN TODAY

Randy Newman is probably the pop world's best-loved misanthrope, an irony that extends quite naturally to his stark little songs, with their honest and often stinging perceptions of a world—an America, mainly—teetering on the borders of love, hate, comedy, tragedy, sanity, madness. A Los Angeles native, and the privileged nephew of Hollywood composer-conductors Lionel, Alfred, and Emil Newman, Randy Newman grew up, by his own account, an unhappy fat boy with crossed eyes and a seemingly terminal inferiority complex. Forged from such an unfelicitous point of view, his lyrics are as apt to be misunderstood at face value as applauded for their surgical incisiveness. Indeed, his 1977 hit "Short People" was thought by many to constitute an unredeemed slur, although the lyric is one of the best ironic indictments of blind prejudice ever written. Newman's relentless irony, of course, is the touchstone of his humor, although one of his most famous lyrics—"I Think It's Going to Rain Today," from his 1968 debut album—is but bleakly ironic. Here, the singer's sense of urban emptiness, hypocrisy, and indifference toward the "Lonely, lonely" seems to extend from the "broken windows" to the "pale dead moon in a sky streaked with gray," and from the "frozen smiles" of "scarecrows dressed in the latest styles" to a feel-it-in-my-bones premonition of rain, poetry's eternal symbol of sadness and the pervasiveness of memory. The bitter lines "Human kindness is overflowing" and "That's the way to treat a friend" suggest a depth of disillusion and disappointment amidst a liberal '60s landscape where "the signs implore" even the lost ones to "help the needy and show them the way."

I THINK IT'S GOING TO RAIN TODAY

Broken windows and empty hallways
A pale dead moon in a sky streaked with gray
Human kindness is overflowing
And I think it's going to rain today

Scarecrows dressed in the latest styles
With frozen smiles to chase love away
Human kindness is overflowing
And I think it's going to rain today

Lonely, lonely
Tin can at my feet
Think I'll kick it down the street
That's the way to treat a friend

Bright before me the signs implore me
Help the needy and show them the way
Human kindness is overflowing
And I think it's going to rain today

Van Morrison

AND IT STONED ME

Summer, 1969: Peacefully and incredibly, a half-million American youths celebrate themselves with music at the Woodstock rock festival in upstate New York. Woodstock reflects the communal hippie spirit at its positive peak, a demonstration of alternative values and survivalist sharing, an ocean of humanity under heavy rains, a wedding of good earth to a mass ideal that seems to promise a new Edenic age, despite the dark violent undertone that co-exists with '60s flower-power. Joni Mitchell's "Woodstock" celebrated the celebration, and it became the almost official retrospective song; but Van Morrison's "And It Stoned Me," from his 1970 album *Moondance,* was the anthem that really seemed to capture the moment.

The lyric is more a memory of idyllic childhood than a meditation on Woodstock. And yet Morrison—the brooding Irish rock-poet whose jazzy vocals widened stylistic channels for a generation of rock singers—seemed to have gotten the range of the Woodstock spirit, its new-eyed affirmation of life, with such beatific lines as "Oh the water/ Let it run all over me." The chorus—"And it stoned me/ . . . just like goin' home"—was obviously in tune with the reality of the drug scene, but Morrison was talking as much about the high of a transcendent feeling, the joy of golden moments in time, the intoxicating sense of connection to earth, air, water, brother, sister.

AND IT STONED ME

Half a mile from the county fair
And the rain came pourin' down
Me and Billy standin' there
With a silver half a crown
Hands were full of fishin' rods
And the tackle on our backs
We just stood there gettin' wet
With our backs against the fence

Oh the water
Hope it don't rain all day
And it stoned me to my soul
Stoned me just like jellyroll
And it stoned me
And it stoned me to my soul
Stoned me just like goin' home
And it stoned me

And the rain let up and the sun came up
And we were gettin dry
Almost glad a pickup truck
Nearly passed us by
So we jumped right in
And the driver grinned
And he dropped us up the road
And we looked at the swim
And we jumped right in
Not to mention fishin' poles

Oh the water
Let it run all over me
And it stoned me to my soul
Stoned me just like jellyroll
And it stoned me
Stoned me just like goin' home
And it stoned me

On the way back home
We sang a song
But our throats were gettin' dry
Then we saw the man from across the road
With the sunshine in his eye

Well he lived all alone in his own little home
With a great big gallon jar
There were bottles too, one for me and you
And he said, 'Hey, there you are'

Oh the water
Get it myself from the mountain stream
And it stoned me to my soul
Stoned me just like jellyroll
And it stoned me
And it stoned me to my soul
Stoned me just like goin' home
And it stoned me

David Ackles

MONTANA SONG

The music and words of David Ackles seem almost too classically influenced and overtly "poetic" to succeed with the pop audience, although this richly gifted singer-songwriter-composer generated considerable interest in the early '70s. His undisputed masterpiece, *American Gothic,* came in 1972—an album so ambitious it sparked comparison to The Beatles's *Sgt. Pepper* but ultimately stood on its own terms as an aural experience of great intensity. It echoed Copland, Gershwin, and *Oklahoma!,* incorporated everything from jazz to gospel—all seamlessly bound to a frame of contemporary pop-rock —and isolated a vast cross-section of Anglo-American experience, blending the vagaries, traditions, and morés of past and present into a magically detailed miniature.

"Montana Song," which ends the album, unites two generations at opposite ends of the American Dream, locating their thread of common spirit and affirming a cosmic unity. The lyric's narrative dimension, meditative intensity, and metric precision set it apart from most efforts in the pop-rock vein, but at the time of its appearance in '72, it seemed to jibe perfectly with rock's evolving interest in the imagery of the Old West and its relation to a new pioneer spirit.

MONTANA SONG

I went out to Montana
With a bible on my arm,
Looking for my fathers
On a long-abandoned farm,
And I found what I came looking for.

I drove into a churchyard
Of what used to be the town;
Walked along a cowpath
Through the fences falling down,
'Til I found what I came looking for.

Through the dust of summer noons,
Over grass long dying,
To read the stone and lumber runes
Where my past was lying.
High among hillsides and windmill bones,
Soft among oak trees and chimney stones,
Blew the wind that I came looking for.

And the wind blew over the dry land,
And dusted my city soul clean,
To read in my great-grandfather's hand
From his bible newly seen:

Born James McKennon, 1862
Married Leantha, 1884
Two sons born in Montana,
Praise the Lord!

The gentle wind of passing time,
Closed the bible pages;
And took my hand
And had me climb
Closer to the ages.

The picket fence, the lattice frame,
The garden gone to seed;
Leantha with the fragile name,
Defying place and need,
Declares this bit of prairie "tame,"

And sees her fingers bleed;
And knows her sons won't live the same,
But she must live her creed.

The fallen barn, the broken plow,
The hoofprint-hardened clay;
Where is the farmer now,
Who built his dream this way?
Who felled the tree and cut the bough
And made the land obey;
Who taught his sons as he knew how,
But could not make them stay.
Who watched until the darkness fell
To know the boys were gone,
And never loved the land so well
From that day on.

"Father James," they wrote him,
Each a letter once a year;
Words of change that broke him
With the new age that was here,
And the new world they'd gone looking for.

The clouds arose
Like phantom herds,
And by the dappled lighting
I read again
The last few words
In a woman's writing:

March 1st, 1921.
Last night, Papa died.
Left one plow, a horse, his gun,
This bible and his bride.

The long grass moved beside me
In the gentle summer rain,
And made a path to guide me
To a sudden mound of grain.

A man and wife are buried there,
Children to the land;
With young green tendrils in her hair,
And seedlings in his hand.

I went out to Montana
With a bible on my arm,
Looking for my fathers
On a long-abandoned farm,
And I found what I came looking for.

David Bowie

ALL THE MADMEN

David Bowie emerged as the 1970s' most original, most elusive rock artist, the one who best understood the logic and illogic of manipulating pop images, anticipating pop trends, and sketching future landscapes that the rock 'n' rollers of the 1980s are still filling in. Bowie's power of suggestion—as a bisexual icon of '70s "new sexuality," as a stagecrafty mime and prophet/proponent of "glitter-rock," of white disco-soul music, of eclectic "new wave" forms —has never failed to compel his audience, nor has it suggested quite enough to allow for his easy categorization. By the same token, Bowie's lyrics are so effective because they often seem to be withholding some vital information that would complete a profoundly sketchy scene—only to defuse it. As if distilled from an intensely fragmented consciousness, Bowie's words are a sheer electric poetry of original thought, arty reference, esoteric philosophy, Dylanesque allusion, and trendy talk. Their flickering immediacy is their grandest illusion, though, for they are in essence timelessly romantic and deeply moral in their vision of a humanity assaulted by images and benighted by technology.

In his 1971 album *The Man Who Sold the World,* Bowie's lyrics rode molten, metallic rock textures to symbolize the numbing intensities of internal and external psycho-pressure, and the album's most disturbing lyric, "All the Madmen," makes a chilling, sardonic identification with the insane. The implication here is that "the madmen," whose "organic minds" represent the pure potential and unrepressed vision of the true artist, are somehow the sane men of a truly insane world, as opposed to the defused, desensitized "sadmen roaming free." This notion was not without precedent or popularity in the 60s, particularly among followers of the psycho-

96

philosopher R. D. Laing. Bowie's lyric, laced with grim irony, raises the question of who and what is sane, and suggests the price of freedom, from the ambivalent point of view he had begun to master. The esoteric chant that ends the song—"Zane Zane Zane/ Ouvre le chien"—suggests some communal transcendence of the rational, the logical, the unliberated literal.

ALL THE MADMEN

Day after day,
They send my friends away
To mansions cold and gray
To the far side of town
Where the thinmen stalk the streets
While the sane stay underground.

Day after day,
They tell me I can go
They tell me I can blow
To the far side of town
Where it's pointless to be high
'Cause it's such a long way down
So I tell them that,
I can fly, I will scream, I will break my arm
I will do me harm
Here I stand, foot in hand, talking to my wall
I'm not quite right at all . . . am I?

Don't set me free, I'm as heavy as can be
Just my Librium and me
And my E. S. T. makes three.

'Cause I'd rather stay here
With all the madmen
Than perish with the sadmen roaming free
And I'd rather play here
With all the madmen
For I'm quite content
They're all as sane as me.

(Where can the horizon lie
When a nation hides
Its organic minds
In a cellar . . . dark and grim
They must be very dim)

Day after day,
They take some brain away
They turn my face around
To the far side of town
And tell me that it's real
Then ask me how I feel.

Here I stand, foot in hand, talking to my wall
I'm not quite right at all.

Don't set me free, I'm as helpless as can be
My libido's split on me
Gimmee some good ole lobotomy.

'Cause I'd rather stay here
With all the madmen
Than perish with the sadmen roaming free
And I'd rather play here
With all the madmen
For I'm quite content
They're all as sane as me.

Zane, Zane, Zane
Ouvre le chien

Bernie Taupin and Elton John

WHERE TO NOW, ST. PETER?

A great measure of Elton John's success in the 1970s was written in the lyrics of Bernie Taupin, the longtime other, and often better, half of John's music. For most of the decade, as before it, Taupin's words rode John's schmaltzy pop-rock constructions in all their brilliance, glory, maudlin excess, and yet retained enough inner character to matter as much as the melody. Taupin wrote with a casually refined British formalism that made up in clarity of expression and elegance of clue whatever it may have lacked in free-flowingness, and at his most visionary, he saw and said a lot without stretching a single metric or metaphoric seam.

"Where to Now, St. Peter?," from 1971's album *Tumbleweed Connection,* isn't one of Taupin's most-remembered lyrics; it isn't one of John's most-remembered songs—but it is one of their best. Is the soldier dreaming of his end, or has he already met it? The reality isn't important here; it's the "blue canoe" floating "like a leaf," the "Half enchanted . . . Merlin sleep," then the mad dawning as "Insane they took the paddles/ My arms they paralysed." These images evoke their twilight zone in a few spare masterstrokes. The chorus asks its anxious agnostic question, and the lyric turns, finally, from poignant philosophy ("It took a sweet young foreign gun/ This lazy life is short") to fatalistic wordplay (" "Something for nothing always ending/With a bad report").

WHERE TO NOW, ST. PETER?

I took myself a blue canoe
And I floated like a leaf
Dazzling, dancing,
Half enchanted
In my Merlin sleep

Crazy was the feeling
Restless were my eyes
Insane they took the paddles
My arms they paralysed

So, where to now, St. Peter
If it's true I'm in your hands
I may not be a Christian
But I've done all one man can
I understand I'm on the road
Where all that was is gone
So where to now, St. Peter
Show me which road I'm on
Which road I'm on

It took a sweet young foreign gun
This lazy life is short
Something for nothing always ending
With a bad report

Dirty was the daybreak
Sudden was the change
In such a silent place as this
Beyond the rifle range.

John Prine

SAM STONE

John Prine enjoyed an almost literally overnight success after he was spotted performing in a Chicago club and, not long after, signed by Atlantic Records. His 1971 debut album hit the airwaves immediately and won over the important critics, who generally hailed him as the latest in a line of "new Dylans"—all of which seemed to obscure the fact that Prine had spent more of his life in the Army and as a postman than as a troubador. But if he seemed to have avoided the lengthy dues-paying of most singer-songwriters, his songs revealed a depth of bittersweet feeling and bardic wisdom well beyond his years. Working in a rustic and understated country vein, Prine etched indelible portraits of an America that seemed to have survived the turbulent '60s at the expense of shattered ideals, to the extent it had survived at all.

"Sam Stone" is Prine's great indictment of our imperialist wars— of Vietnam, mainly—although its power as a lyric does not derive from any ardent, Dylanesque rhetoric of protest. Instead, we respond to its quiet personalization of a broken soldier, his drug addiction, the helplessness of his family, and society's indifference. The laconic rhythm of Prine's poetry has an almost throwaway feel, but here his key conceit, "sweet songs never last too long on broken radios," gets the range of American illusion and reality as potently as anything Dylan ever sang.

SAM STONE

Sam Stone came home
To his wife and family
After serving in the conflict overseas
And the time that he served
Had shattered all his nerves
And left a little shrapnel in his knee
But the morphine eased the pain
And the grass grew round his brain
And gave him all the confidence he lacked
With a purple heart and a monkey on his back

There's a hole in daddy's arm
Where all the money goes
And Jesus Christ died for nothing
I suppose
Little pitchers have big ears
Don't stop to count the years
Sweet songs never last too long
On broken radios

Sam Stone's welcome home
Didn't last too long
He went to work when he'd spent his last dime
And Sammy took to stealing
When he got that empty feeling
For a hundred dollar habit, without overtime
And the gold rolled through his veins
Like a thousand railroad trains
And eased his mind in the hours that he chose

There's a hole in daddy's arm
Where all the money goes
And Jesus Christ died for nothing
I suppose
Little pitchers have big ears
Don't stop to count the years
Sweet songs never last too long
On broken radios.

HELLO IN THERE

Another highlight of John Prine's 1971 debut album, "Hello in There" is one of the few lyrics about old age that manages to be personal and poignant without stooping to easy sentiment. Prine's old folks accept the reality of their neglected, diminished lives—lives drained of purpose, circumstance, conversation—and they have transferred their ineffable longing to a simple act of acknowledgment. The imagery is sparse—like gray hair on a nearly bald old head—but the poetry offers the clues of time, place, and temperament ("She sits and stares thru the back door screen") that locate and define this small universe of loss.

HELLO IN THERE

We had an apartment in the city
And me and Loretta liked living there
It'd been years since the kids had grown
A life of their own
And left us alone
John and Linda live in Omaha
And Joe is somewhere on the road
We lost Davy in the Korean War
I still don't know what for
Don't matter anymore

Ya know, that old trees just grow stronger
And old rivers grow wilder everyday
Old people just grow lonesome
Waiting for someone to say
Hello in there
Hello

Me and Loretta, we don't talk much more
She sits and stares thru the back door screen
And all the news just repeats itself
Like some forgotten dream
That we've both seen
Someday I'll go and call up Rudy
We worked together at the factory
But what could I say when he asked "What's new?"
Nothing, what's with you?
Nothing much to do

So if you're walking down the street sometime
And spot some hollow ancient eyes
Please don't just pass 'em by and stare
As if you didn't care
Say hello in there
Hello

THE GREAT COMPROMISE

This lyric, from his 1972 album *Diamonds in the Rough,* metaphorically perfects the homely sense of national disillusion articulated by John Prine in the early '70s. Here, the singer's sense of betrayal —by a beautiful, beguiling woman and, in the larger sense, by his beautiful, beguiling country—is conveyed with the sort of joke's-on-me wit and gritty realism that elevates the transparent double entendre of the lyric well above any mere technical exercise. Prine's two-timing heroine is "a girl who was almost a lady/ . . . born on the fourth of July," and she lives "in an aluminum house trailer" and works "in a jukebox saloon." Her romanticism is awesome, overreaching, endearing—"And she spent all the money I give her/ Just to see the old man in the moon"—but she only shatters faith when she hops "into a foreign sports car."

The symbolism relates, of course, to America's moon-walking greatness on one hand, its ignoble involvement in Vietnam on the other. But the singer's moral stance has nothing to do with countercultural protest. "I could have beat up that fellow/ But it was her that hopped into his car," he explains, and though "Many times I'd fought to protect her," he won't "fight for a thing that ain't right." Here is just the sort of innocent integrity we associate with the American experience. And here, in the rude awakening of the song's chorus, is its price.

THE GREAT COMPROMISE

I knew a girl who was almost a lady
She had a way with all the men in her life
Every inch of her blossomed in beauty
And she was born on the fourth of July
Well she lived in an aluminum house trailer
And she worked in a jukebox saloon
And she spent all the money I give her
Just to see the old man in the moon.

I used to sleep at the foot of Old Glory
And awake in the dawn's early light
But much to my surprise
When I opened my eyes
I was a victim of the great compromise.

Well we'd go out on Saturday evenings
To the drive-in on Route 41
And it was there that I first suspected
That she was doin' what she'd already done
She said "Johnny won't you get me some popcorn"
And she knew I had to walk pretty far
And as soon as I passed through the moonlight
She hopped into a foreign sports car.

I used to sleep at the foot of Old Glory
And awake in the dawn's early light
But much to my surprise
When I opened my eyes
I was a victim of the great compromise.

Well you know I could have beat up that fellow
But it was her that hopped into his car
Many times I'd fought to protect her
But this time she was goin' too far
Now some folks they call me a coward
'Cause I left her at the drive-in that night
But I'd druther have names thrown at me
Than to fight for a thing that ain't right.

I used to sleep at the foot of Old Glory
And awake in the dawn's early light
But much to my surprise

When I opened my eyes
I was a victim of the great compromise.

Now she writes all the fellows love letters
Saying "Greetings, come and see me real soon"
And they go and line up in the barroom
And spend the night in that sick woman's room
But sometimes I get awful lonesome
And I wish she was my girl instead
But she won't let me live with her
And she makes me live in my head.

I used to sleep at the foot of Old Glory
And awake in the dawn's early light
But much to my surprise
When I opened my eyes
I was a victim of the great compromise.

Billy Joel

SCENES FROM AN ITALIAN RESTAURANT

Billy Joel rode out the 1970s as urban America's great balladeer, straight-shooting, streetwise, modestly middle-class, with all the wit, craft, polish, and passion to redefine pop-rock in his own image. Joel's mass-appeal romanticism of the regular guy succeeded the Anglo flowerings of Elton John, and Paul McCartney, whose ripe, hook-laden melodies he echoed. With *The Stranger* in 1977, Joel came into his own as a lyricist—and only coincidentally as a major star —with words that held effortlessly to his perfect melodies yet stood on their own as sharply inventive conversational miniatures, straight from the heart of a hard-boiled American dream that still hadn't lost its faith in love or the future.

"Scenes from an Italian Restaurant" is the album's epic, a cynic's chronicle of star high school sweethearts whose post-graduate love can't quite go the distance. Here, Joel sets scenes with the unsparing graphic economy of the true raconteur ("They got an apartment with deep/ Pile carpet/ And a couple of paintings from Sears") and yet the whole vision is conjured from a bittersweet ambivalence toward the past and present ("A bottle of white, A bottle of red/ Perhaps a bottle of rose instead/ We'll get a table near the street/ In our old familiar place")—as if good times only exist in retrospect.

SCENES FROM AN ITALIAN RESTAURANT

A bottle of white, A bottle of red
Perhaps a bottle of rose instead
We'll get a table near the street
In our old familiar place
You and I—Face to face
A bottle of red, a bottle of white
It all depends upon your appetite
I'll meet you any time you want
In our Italian Restaurant.
Things are okay with me these days
Got a good job, got a good office
Got a new wife, got a new life
And the family's fine
We lost touch long ago
You lost weight I did not know
You could ever look so good after
So much time.
I remember those days hanging out
At the village green
Engineer boots, leather jackets
And tight blue jeans
Drop a dime in the box play the
Song about New Orleans
Cold beer, hot lights
My sweet romantic teenage nights.
Brenda and Eddie were the
Popular steadies
And the king and the queen
Of the prom
Riding around with the car top
Down and the radio on
Nobody looked any finer
Or was more of a hit at the
Parkway Diner
We never knew we could want more
Than that out of life
Surely Brenda and Eddie would
Always know how to survive.
Brenda and Eddie were still going
Steady in the summer of '75

When they decided the marriage would
Be at the end of July
Everyone said they were crazy
"Brenda you know you're much too lazy
Eddie could never afford to live that kind of life"
But there we were wavin' Brenda and
Eddie goodbye.
They got an apartment with deep
Pile carpet
And a couple of paintings from Sears
A big waterbed that they bought
With the bread
They had saved for a couple
Of years
They started to fight when the
Money got tight
And they just didn't count on the tears.
They lived for a while in a
Very nice style
But it's always the same in the end
They got a divorce as a matter
Of course
And they parted the closest of friends
Then the king and the queen went
Back to the green
But you can never go back there again.
Brenda and Eddie had had it
Already by the summer of '75
From the high to the low to
The end of the show
For the rest of their lives
They couldn't go back to the greasers
The best they could do
Was pick up the pieces
We always knew they would both
Find a way to get by
That's all I heard about Brenda and Eddie
Can't tell you more than I
Told you already
And here we are wavin' Brenda
And Eddie goodbye.
A bottle of red, A bottle of white

Whatever kind of mood you're
In tonight
I'll meet you anytime you want
In our Italian Restaurant.

Bruce Springsteen

LOST IN THE FLOOD

1973: The songs crackled on the radio with all the energy of some new motor-mad Dylan, a jubilant rush of words, melody, urgent meaning. Bred in the backyards of the East Coast, here was Bruce Springsteen, a new voice out of home town Freehold, New Jersey, by way of seaside Asbury Park, a rock 'n' roller *par excellence* who'd kicked around the clubs and bars, with his evolving E-Street Band, long enough to be thought of as a grizzled veteran. In fact, he was still in his early twenties, but now he'd been signed to CBS Records —after one audition, goes the legend—by the great John Hammond, who had done much the same for Bob Dylan a decade earlier.

Springsteen's first album, *Greetings from Asbury Park,* made true believers out of most who heard it, although it would take him two more albums to crack the pop charts. Still, there was no mistaking the richness of his music or the brilliance of his lyrics, with their breathless compression, playful assonance, freewheeling metaphor, and visionary intensity—lyrics evocative of Dylan's, but strikingly original at the same time.

"Lost in the Flood" stands as the most disturbing and dimensional of the songs on Bruce Springsteen's first album. Its imagery blazes with strangely sensible Dylanisms—"The ragamuffin gunner . . ./ His countryside's burnin' with/ Wolfman fairies dressed in/ Drag for homicide . . ."—while its narrative flows from the chaos of some imagined civil war, to the realities of stock-car racing and shoot-outs between cops and street gangs. The lyric says a lot about our fascination with violence and conjures the romance of dying young and in one's own style rather than washing out with all the others, lost in the flood. It's an apocalyptic song about everyday endings of the world.

113

LOST IN THE FLOOD

The ragamuffin gunner is
Returnin' home like a hungry runaway
He walks through town all alone
He must be from the fort he hears
The high school girls say
His countryside's burnin' with
Wolfman fairies dressed in
Drag for homicide
They hit and run, plead sanctuary,
'Neath a holy stone they hide
They're breakin' beams and
Crosses with a spastic's reelin'
Perfection
Nuns run bald through Vatican
Halls pregnant, pleadin'
Immaculate conception
And everybody's wrecked on
Main Street from drinking
Unholy blood
Sticker smiles sweet as gunner
Breathes deep, his ankles
Caked in mud
And I said, "Hey, gunner man,
That's quicksand, that's
Quicksand that ain't mud
Have you thrown your senses
To the war or did you lose them
In the flood?"

That pure American brother,
Dull-eyed and empty-faced
Races Sundays in Jersey in a
Chevy stocked super eight
He rides 'er low on the hip, on
The side he's got Bound
For Glory in red, white and
Blue flash paint
He leans on the hood telling
Racing stories, the kids call him
Jimmy the Saint
Well that blaze and noise boy,

He's gunnin' that bitch loaded
To blastin' point
He rides head first into a
Hurricane and disappears into
A point
And there's nothin' left but some
Blood where the body fell
And there's nothin' left that you
Could sell
Just junk all across the horizon,
A real highwayman's farewell
And I said, "Hey kid, you think
That's oil? Man, that ain't oil
That's blood."
I wonder what he was thinking
When he hit that storm
Or was he just lost in the flood?

Eighth Avenue sailors in satin
Shirts whisper in the air
Some storefront incarnation of
Maria, she's puttin' on me
The stare
And Bronx's best apostle stands
With his hand on his own
Hardware
Everything stops, you hear five,
Quick shots, the cops come
Up for air
And now the whiz-bang gang
From uptown, they're shootin'
Up the street
And that cat from the Bronx
Starts lettin' loose
But he gets blown right off his feet
And some kid comes blastin'
Round the corner but a cop
Puts him right away
He lays on the street holding his
Leg screaming something in
Spanish
Still breathing when I walked away
And somebody said, "Hey man

Did you see that? His body hit
The street with such a beautiful
Thud."
I wonder what the dude was
Sayin' or was he just lost in
The flood?
Hey man, did you see that,
Those poor cats are sure
Messed up
I wonder what they were
Gettin' into, or were they just
Lost in the flood?

BACKSTREETS

Born to Run was the album—his third—that did the trick for Bruce Springsteen. No sooner was it released in 1975 than Springsteen made the covers of *Time* and *Newsweek* magazines in the same week —an unparalleled feat for a musician. Understandably, the album took off and vaulted up the pop charts, but detractors called it all a hype, Springsteen another great pretender. The album itself spoke differently. These were songs of exceptional force, their sound inspired by Phil Spector's oceanic rock productions of the early '60s, a vivid American romance forged somewhere between *West Side Story* and the war in Vietnam.

"Well, that's the idea. There's a lot of different sides to it," Springsteen told me in 1978, during a tumultuous concert tour. He was reflecting on the impact and influence of Spector's "wall-of-sound" style. "It's an onslaught, an affront—it's like a personal affront. It's just like an attack and it's beautiful and it's gentle and it's funny sometimes, and it's innocent and it's like . . . it's like a little guy that just—boom!—shook up the world." Springsteen's description fits *Born to Run* as truly as it does Spector's style. Here were songs of the outlaw and the angel in every teenager, anthems of brief escape from boring jobs into the endlessly promising night, of stock-car cowboys, kid desperadoes, sad, beautiful girls, manifestos of street pride, wails of survival. "Backstreets" is one of the album's most potent lyrics; nostalgic but far from sentimental, its voice is passionately alive to the past and to "the truth that ran us down." Its anguish is the legacy of the dead-end kid, and of the dead-end kid in anyone who ever sought refuge in a world that seemed to belong to someone else.

BACKSTREETS

One soft infested summer
Me and Terry became friends
Tryin' in vain to breathe
The fire we was born in
Catching rides to the outskirts
Tying faith between our teeth
Sleeping in that old abandoned beach house
Getting wasted in the heat
And hiding on the backstreets
Hiding on the backstreets
With a love so hard and filled with defeat
Running for our lives at night on them backstreets.

Slow dancing in the dark
On the beach at Stockton's Wing
Where desperate lovers park
We sat with the last of the Duke Street Kings
Huddled in our cars
Waiting for the bells that ring
In the deep heart of the night
We let loose of everything
To go running on the backstreets
Running on the backstreets
Terry, you swore we'd live forever
Taking it on them backstreets together.

Endless juke joints and Valentino drag
Where dancers scraped the tears
Up off the street dressed down in rags
Running into the darkness
Some hurt bad some really dying
At night sometime it seemed
You could hear the whole damn city crying
Blame it on the lies that killed us
Blame it on the truth that ran us down
You can blame it all on me, Terry
It don't matter to me now
When the breakdown hit at midnight
There was nothing left to say
But I hated him
And I hated you when you went away.

Laying here in the dark
You're like an angel on my chest
Just another tramp of hearts
Crying tears of faithlessness
Remember all the movies, Terry
We'd go see
Trying to learn how to walk like the heroes
We thought we had to be
And after all this time
To find we're just like all the rest
Stranded in the park
And forced to confess
To hiding on the backstreets
Hiding on the backstreets
Where we swore forever friends
On the backstreets until the end.

JUNGLELAND

"Jungleland" is the lavish finale of *Born to Run*—a giant, theatrical song that evokes "an opera out on the turnpike/ . . . a ballet being fought out in the alley," as the "hungry and the hunted/ Explode into rock 'n' roll bands." This fantasy of street and city, where the law of the jungle still prevails, is etched in Springsteen's finest poetry and locates a space in time where only action speaks ("And the poets down here/ Don't write nothin' at all/ They just stand back and let it all be"—a magnificent line) and where "no one watches" as the action fades into brief, blessed peace.

JUNGLELAND

The Rangers had a homecoming
In Harlem late last night
And the Magic Rat drove his sleek machine
Over the Jersey state line
Barefoot girl sitting on the hood of a Dodge
Drinking warm beer in the soft summer rain
The Rat pulls into town rolls up his pants
Together they take a stab at romance
And disappear down Flamingo Lane.

Well the Maximum Lawman run down Flamingo
Chasing the Rat and the barefoot girl
And the kids 'round here look just like shadows
Always quiet holding hands
From the churches to the jails
Tonight all is silence in the world
As we take our stand
Down in Jungleland.

The midnight gang's assembled
And picked a rendezvous for the night
They'll meet 'neath that giant Exxon sign
That brings this fair city light
Man there's an opera out on the turnpike
There's a ballet being fought out in the alley
Until the local cops
Cherry Tops
Rips this holy night
The street's alive
As secret debts are paid
Contacts made they vanish unseen
Kids flash guitars just like switchblades
Hustling for the record machine
The hungry and the hunted
Explode into rock 'n' roll bands
That face off against each other out in the street
Down in Jungleland.

In the parking lot the visionaries
Dress in the latest rage
Inside the backstreet girls are dancing
To the records that the DJ plays

Lonely-hearted lovers
Struggle in dark corners
Desperate as the night moves on
Just one look
A whisper, and they're gone.

Beneath the city two hearts beat
Soul engines running through a night so tender
In a bedroom locked
In whispers of soft refusal
And then surrender
In the tunnels uptown
The Rat's own dream guns him down
As shots echo down the hallways in the night
No one watches as the ambulance pulls away
Or as the girl shuts out the bedroom light.

Outside the street's on fire
In a real death waltz
Between what's flesh and what's fantasy
And the poets down here
Don't write nothing at all
They just stand back and let it all be
And in the quick of a knife
They reach for a moment
And try to make an honest stand
But they wind up wounded
Not even dead
Tonight in Jungleland.

DARKNESS ON THE EDGE OF TOWN

1978: After *Born to Run*'s breakthrough, Bruce Springsteen's career would be limboed by a legal struggle for almost three years. He sought release from his original contract with manager/producer Mike Appel, and while the lawyers tangled, Springsteen was largely enjoined from performing and even recording. When he finally did get back in the studio—with Jon Landau co-producing and later managing—the exultant kid-outlaw flash of *Born to Run* had been muted to a somber passion.

Darkness on the Edge of Town was the album, a coming of age for Springsteen, an end to the busy word-spinning style. These new songs were stark and square-measured in their imagery, seething with the soiled frustrations and pure hope of working stiffs, who may have lost their main chance but haven't given up on the big thrills of a rebel life or the big dreams of love, winning, breaking out of the "Badlands" and into "The Promised Land." The music throbbed with timeless echoes of a musical past—from gospel to Chuck Berry, Elvis Presley, and beyond—that ran deeper than Phil Spector's teen-dream concoctions.

"I never considered myself to be a certain kind of innovator," said Springsteen in 1978. "I seek things out that ring true or rang true to me, and then I try to make them real again, for people who maybe didn't get it the first time, plus bring something new to it that comes into my life. Maybe there's a Chuck Berry song, or a book, or something . . . and I say, 'well, okay, now I'm gonna bring that along, and pick out what runs through me and put my stuff into it . . .' " Springsteen imparts a painfully personal quality to the songs of this album, as if there were no longer any point in separating heroes from victims. He reveals himself through his outlaws, outlaws biblically resigned to the fatherhoods of fate ("Adam Raised a Cain"), living "on the line where dreams are found and lost," proud and lonely and brave in "wanting things that can only be found/ In the darkness on the edge . . ." The title song is a great grim gospel, as faith is tested on "a spot out 'neath Abram's Bridge . . ."

DARKNESS ON THE EDGE OF TOWN

They're still racing out at the Trestles,
But that blood it never burned in her veins,
Now I hear she's got a house up in Fairview,
And a style she's trying to maintain.
Well, if she wants to see me,
You can tell her that I'm easily found,
Tell her there's a spot out 'neath Abram's Bridge,
And tell her, there's a darkness on the edge of town.

Everybody's got a secret, Sonny,
Something that they just can't face,
Some folks spend their whole lives trying to keep it,
They carry it with them every step that they take.
Till some day they just cut it loose
Cut it loose or let it drag 'em down,
Where no one asks any questions,
Or looks too long in your face,
In the darkness on the edge of town.

Some folks are born into a good life,
Other folks get it anyway, anyhow,
I lost my money and I lost my wife,
Them things don't seem to matter much to me now.
Tonight I'll be on that hill 'cause I can't stop,
I'll be on that hill with everything I got,
Lives on the line where dreams are found and lost,
I'll be there on time and I'll pay the cost,
For wanting things that can only be found
In the darkness on the edge of town.

Lowell George and Little Feat

WILLIN'

From their pop beginnings in 1970 to their swan song in 1979 upon the death of leader and figurehead Lowell George, Little Feat was one of America's most admirable and admired bands. Drawing on a lowdown country-blues base, the group rocked with a laconic sophistication that seemed to celebrate the persistent cult of the hippie outlaw, cynical of institutions and wisely, romantically alive to the truckers, bikers, and loose-livers who symbolized some new American Dream of modest, mobile resourcefulness. George's songwriting set the tone, of course, and his best lyric is probably "Willin'," a trucker's declaration of independence—and faith—from Little Feat's 1972 album *Sailin' Shoes.* With its alliterative inventory of dusty backroad odysseys("from tucson to/ tucumcari/ from tehachapi to tonopah"), its sense of endless fatigue relieved by "weed,/ whites and wine," and of ultimate willingness to obey "a sign" (an invitation to love? or just another highway sign?), this insistently lower-case lyric pictures someone locked into a life of dissipation and distant reward—and loving it.

WILLIN'

i was out on the road late at
night
seen my pretty alice in every
headlight
alice dallas alice
i been warped by the rain,
driven by
the snow drunk and dirty don't
you know
and i'm still willin'

i've been from tucson to
tucumcari
from tehachapi to tonopah
driven every
kind of rig that's ever been
made driven
the back roads so I wouldn't get
weighed
and if you give me weed,
whites and wine
and show me a sign i'll be
willin'

i've been kicked by the wind,
robbed by the
sleet had my head stoved in
but i'm still on
my feet and i'm still willin'
i smuggled some smokes and
folks from mexico
baked by the sun every time i
go to mexico
and i'm still willin'

and i've been from tucson to
tucumcari
from tehachapi to tonopah
driven every
kind of rig that's ever been
made driven
the back roads so i wouldn't get

weighed
and if you give me weed,
whites and wine
and show me a sign
i'll be willin'
to be movin'

Neil Diamond

IF YOU KNOW WHAT I MEAN

Neil Diamond rose to the front rank of pop music the hard way, after much frustration and dues-paying as a songwriter on New York's Tin Pan Alley. In 1976, at the peak of his career, he chose to look back and, with a single album, *Beautiful Noise,* co-produced with Robbie Robertson of The Band, reflected on the sprawling tradition of American popsong in general and his own odyssey in particular. The album was primarily a musical milestone, but it contained at least one great lyric. "If You Know What I Mean" managed to express the singer's inexpressible sense of a simpler, sweeter past that he'd given away "for the sake of a dream/ In a penny arcade . . ." The sentiment here is stronger than nostalgia, and maybe more than sentimental. The idea of music as a cultural force pervading and somehow defining intimate lives—"and the radio played like a carnival tune/ As we lay in our bed in the other room . . ."—mingles with a sense of loss profoundly overcome, again, by the music.

IF YOU KNOW WHAT I MEAN

When the night returns just like a friend,
When the evening comes to set me free,
When the quiet hours that wait beyond the day make
Peaceful sounds in me.
Took a drag from my last cigarette,
Took a drink from a glass of old wine,
Closed my eyes and I could make it real and
Feel it one more time.

Can you hear it, babe?
Can you hear it, babe?
From another time, from another place,
Do you remember it, babe?

And the radio played like a carnival tune
As we lay in our bed in the other room,
And we gave it away for the sake of a dream
In a penny arcade,
If you know what I mean.

And here's to the songs we used to sing.
Here's to the times we used to know.
It's hard to hold them in our arms again but
Hard to let them go.

Do you hear it, babe?
Do you hear it, babe?
It was another time, it was another place,
Do you remember it, babe?

And the radio played like a carnival tune
As we lay in our bed in the other room,
And we gave it away for the sake of a dream
In a penny arcade,
If you know what I mean.
If you know what I mean, babe.

James Taylor

CAROLINA IN MY MIND

James Taylor was the only lasting good to come from The Beatles's short-lived Apple recording company of the late 1960s. Signed in 1968 on the basis of a taped demo of his songs, Taylor debuted on Apple, but didn't become a star until he'd left the label and joined Warner Bros. Records with a second album, *Sweet Baby James,* that yielded hit singles—"Fire and Rain," "Country Road"—and established him in the pop mainstream as the honey-voiced troubador of a mellowing rock. Artistically, however, Taylor was more the confessional folk-poet than an AM-radio crooner, and his homespun reluctance to go it as "celebrity" began to define his style almost at the expense of what he had to say. Indeed, anyone who had paid attention to Taylor's gemlike Apple album of 1969 not only recognized the first flowerings of a major songwriter, but discerned a life story of considerable inner turbulence. As these autobiographical songs either suggested or spelled out, James Taylor had come far from his upper-middle-class Boston upbringing in a large, musical family. From a youthful involvement with provincial folk and rock bands, Taylor endured a late-adolescent identity crisis that led his moody self through a stint at a mental hospital, to a serious drug problem, and eventually to the New York folk scene, where he scuffled for a while before making his fateful pilgrimage to London and Apple.

As a lyric, "Carolina in My Mind," from his Apple debut, seems steeped in '60s drug-trippiness, but more than that it clues us in to a deeply felt sense of community and fate; it suggests the spiritual salves of friendship and familiarity pitted against the forces of isolation and strangeness (" . . . with a holy host of others standing 'round me/ Still I'm on the dark side of the moon"). At work here is Taylor's gift for transcendent imagery turned with folksy under-statement ("Karin she's a silver sun/ You'd best walk her way and watch it shine"). The lyric conveys a notion of escape to Everyman's heaven on earth.

CAROLINA IN MY MIND

In my mind I'm gone to Carolina
Can't you see the sunshine
Can't you just feel the moonshine
And ain't it just like a friend of mine
To hit me from behind
And I'm gone to Carolina in my mind

Karin she's a silver sun
You'd best walk her way and watch it shine
Watch her watch the morning come
A silver tear appearing now I'm crying ain't I
Gone to Carolina in my mind

There ain't no doubt in no-one's mind
That love's the finest thing around
Whisper something soft and kind
And hey babe the sky's on fire I'm dying ain't I
Gone to Carolina in my mind

Dark and silent late last night
Think I might have heard the highway call
Geese in flight and dogs that bite
And signs that might be omens say I'm going going
Gone to Carolina in my mind

Now with a holy host of others standing 'round me
Still I'm on the dark side of the moon
And it seems like it goes on like this forever
You must forgive me

In my mind I'm gone to Carolina
Can't you see the sunshine
Can't you just feel the moonshine
And ain't it just like a friend of mine
To hit me from behind
And I'm gone to Carolina in my mind

James Taylor and Carly Simon

TERRA NOVA

1974: James Taylor weds another glamorously moody singer-songwriter, Carly Simon—"the first superstar merger in rock,"—but their marital collaborations produce more than good publicity and two children. In the recording studio and occasionally onstage, James and Carly assist and inspire each other. Their best co-written song is "Terra Nova," a timeless hymn of departure and return set tangibly in the 1977 of James Taylor's album *JT*. The lyric hinges on its imagery of tempered faith ("May this day/ Show me an ocean") and restless delay ("I ought to be on my way right now"), while the singer locates and reveals himself amidst all the inner and outer tides of past, present, future, of love promised and professed, of city-bred temptation, inertia, passivity ("My mind in the gutter/ And my eye on the street/ Holed up in a cave of concrete"). The final verses—sung on the album by Carly Simon, as if telepathically consoling a left-behind husband—relieve the tension by relocating us in the real world ("Out to the west of Lambert's Cove") for a sadder-but-wiser homecoming.

TERRA NOVA

Oh end this day
Show me the ocean
When shall I see the sea?
May this day set me in motion
I ought to be on my way

We were there
We were sailing on the Terra Nova
Sailing for the setting sun
Sailing for the new horizon

May this day
Show me an ocean
I ought to be on my way
Ought to be on my way right now
Stepping on the boat with a lump in my throat
On my way right now

I got a letter from a dear friend of mine
The story of a spiritual awakening
She spoke of her love
Returning in kind
She let me know that she'd be waiting
And I should be on my way by now
Walking across the floor
Reaching for the door
On my way by now

But here I sit
Country fool that I am
My elbow on my knee
And my chin in my hand
My mind in the gutter
And my eye on the street
Holed up in a cave of concrete

And I ought to be on my way right now
Packing my things while the telephone rings
On my way right now

I miss my lovely mother
And I love my lonely father
I know I owe my brothers

One thing and another
I hear my sister singing

And I ought to be on my way right now
Moving 'cross the land with my heart in my hand
On my way by now
Ought to be on my way by now

Oh end this day
Set me in motion
I ought to be on my way

Out to the west of Lambert's Cove
There is a sail out in the sun
And I'm on board though very small
I've come home to stop yearning

Burn off the haze around the shore
Turn off this crazy way I feel
I'll stay away from you no more
I've come home to stop yearning

Heart

MISTRAL WIND

The female energies unleashed by the woman's liberation ethic of the 1960s were bound to find expression in the male-dominated field of rock music. By the end of the '70s, a growing number of female artists were successfully breaking the folkie mold of fragile femininity that had prevailed—with some obvious exceptions—in rock. A good example was Heart, a coed band out of Seattle, Washington, led by the singing, songwriting, and guitar playing of two very charismatic sisters, Ann and Nancy Wilson. The thrust of their appeal lay in a crafty blend of acoustic-folk textures and hard-rock tension, while the lyric drama, as performed with great range, intensity, and bravado by lead singer Ann Wilson, suggested the sort of role-reversal—woman as an aggressively secure rock icon—that hadn't been pulled off as well since the '60s heyday of Janis Joplin, or Grace Slick and Jefferson Airplane. Significantly, Heart's music suggested more than "female macho." At its best, it asserted the eternal interdependence of male and female forces and allowed for a delicate lyricism of feminine sway-and-yield.

Heart's 1978 album, *Dog and Butterfly,* was a most artful exploration of this yin-yang theme, and its most evocative lyric was "Mistral Wind," with its grand metaphor. Here, the mistral wind—the "masterwind," the violent northwest gust of the Mediterranean—represents a masculine power of love to match and master the most independent feminine soul. "I have always held the wheel/ But I let that wind/ Steal my power," confesses the singer, "A restless sailor . . . waiting," who casts for love with "words of will . . ."

MISTRAL WIND

No wind when I took the watch
My ship was still and waiting.
I lay on that mirrored sky
A restless sailor . . . waiting.
I closed my eyes
Said the words of will
For the gentle breathing
That moves the seas
Make my sails fill.

Whisper waves cloud the glass
Awake at last like a lover.
It rushed around me
Talking sweet
"Roll over roll over
Roll over."
And in my ear he blew his name
It sound so strange
But I heard it plain
Mistral wind.

I have always held the wheel
But I let that wind
Steal my power
Let it spin me around
Lose my course
Nights run by like hours.
It showed me the way
To the deepest mountain
Too high too beautiful to be
Mistral wind.

All the hours on the watch
I wait for that breeze
To move me
And blow me back
To that place
Magic space all through me.
And I sigh your name
Across the empty water
You made a crazy dreamer
Out of me
Mistral wind.

Rickie Lee Jones

THE LAST CHANCE TEXACO

Rickie Lee Jones was another female rock artist of the 1970s who managed to succeed on her own terms. From the outset, her image and music suggested an aging, streetwise tomboy with no particular desire to grow up into the adult world of traditional role and responsibility, even though womanhood had already caught up with her. The sweet tension, inventiveness, and jazzy hipsterism of Rickie Lee's songs conveyed a broadly influenced and instinctive American style—she had emigrated from the midwest to the West Coast "promised land" by her early twenties—while her lyrics invoked a conversational poetry rich in revealing metaphor and the elusive details of time and place. "The Last Chance Texaco," from her 1979 debut album, is a lovelorn lyric that ingeniously equates romantic hesitancy with car trouble ("She gets scared and she stalls . . . Her timing's all wrong . . ."). Beyond this intimate poetry, of course, lies a grand metaphor for America's love affair with the car, a symbol of democratic mobility that had already fallen under the shadow of the oil-hungry '80s.

THE LAST CHANCE TEXACO

A long stretch of headlights
Bends into I-9
Tiptoe into truck stops
And sleepy diesel eyes
Volcanoes rumble in the taxi
And glow in the dark
Camels in the driver's seat
A slow, easy mark

But you ran out of gas
Down the road apiece,
Then the battery went dead
And now the cable won't reach . . .

It's your last chance
To check under the hood,
Last chance
She ain't soundin' too good,
Your last chance
To Trust the Man with the Star
You've found the Last Chance Texaco

Well, he tried to be Standard
He tried to be Mobil
He tried living in a World
And in a Shell
There was this block-busted blonde
He loved her—free parts and labor,
But she broke down and died
And threw all the rods he gave her

But this one ain't fuel-injected,
Her plug's disconnected
She gets scared and she stalls
She just needs a man, that's all

It's her last chance
Her timing's all wrong
Her last chance
She can't idle this long
Her last chance
Turn her over and go
Pullin' out of the Last Chance Texaco
The last chance . . .